24 ADAMSVILLE - COLLIER HEIGHTS

You Can Experience . . .

A Purposeful Life

You Can Experience . . .

A Purposeful Life

by

James Emery White

WORD PUBLISHING

NASHVILLE

A Thomas Nelson Company

Unless otherwise noted, Scripture references are from the Holy Bible: New International Version®. Copyright © 1973, 1978, 1984 by International Bible Society. Used by permission of Zondervan Publishing House. All rights reserved.

Other Scripture references are from the following sources:

The Living Bible (TLB), copyright © 1971 by Tyndale House Publishers, Wheaton, Illinois. Used by permission.

The Message (MSG), copyright ©1993. Used by permission of NavPress Publishing Group.

The Holy Bible, New Century Version (NCV), copyright © 1987, 1988, 1991 by Word Publishing. All rights reserved.

J. B. Phillips: The New Testament in Modern English, Revised Edition (PHILLIPS). Copyright © J. B. Phillips 1958, 1960, 1972. Used by permission of Macmillan Publishing Co., Inc.

The Good News Bible: The Bible in Today's English Version (TEV) © 1976 by the American Bible Society.

The Holy Bible, New Living Translation (NLT), Copyright © 1996. Used by permission of Tyndale House Publishers, Inc., Wheaton, Illinois. All rights reserved.

New American Standard Bible (NASB), © 1960, 1977 by the Lockman Foundation.

Library of Congress Cataloging-in-Publication Data

White, James Emery, 1961–
    You can experience—a purposeful life / James Emery White.
        p. cm.
    Includes bibliographical references.
    ISBN 0-8499-3767-1
    1. Christian life. 2. Life—Religious aspects—Christianity. I. Title.
BV4501.2 .W44918 2000
248.4—dc21

99-088466
CIP

Printed in the United States of America
00 01 02 03 04 05 06 PHX 9 8 7 6 5 4 3 2

Acknowledgments

I am indebted to my assistant, Devlin McNeil, who selflessly serves me in so many ways, as well as to the good folks of Mecklenburg Community Church, who selflessly put up with me in so many ways. I also want to thank the team at Word Publishing for their vision and support, particularly Mark Sweeney, Ami McConnell, and Jennifer Stair. As always, the greatest thanks goes to my wife, Susan, who once again made every page possible.

To Rebecca, Rachel, Jonathan, and Zachary:
May each of you find and follow your purpose in life,
and, by God's grace,
may I be there for you every step of the way.

Contents

Introduction

Some books are written because they fill a particular void, others because they speak to a current issue. Still others, often the best, are written out of an author's passion. I am under no illusions that this book is to be marked among the best, but it was certainly written with an author's passion.

There are many books on purposeful living, yet most seem to fall into one of four camps: those that reduce a purposeful life to nothing but spiritual gifts and natural abilities, those that make a purposeful life little more than a well-managed life, those that limit a purposeful life to the fulfillment of personal dreams and individual success, and those that make a purposeful life simply the search for the situational or moral will of God. All four types, by *themselves*, fall short. I am convinced that experiencing a purposeful life involves each of these elements—and more. It is my hope and prayer that this book brings together the many dynamics of finding and following your life purpose.

— James Emery White
Charlotte, North Carolina

Chapter One

The Life You Long For

Steve always dreamed of his own business and financial success. But more than that, Steve truly believed in his dream to have computers—*personal* computers—in every home and in every office, affordable to all. He knew that such technology placed in the hands of men and women, boys and girls, would revolutionize the world. So Steve took the step of establishing himself as chairman of a start-up computer company. But before long he realized that, while he knew *computers,* for his dream to be realized, he would need someone who knew *business.* Wanting the best available CEO for his young company, Steve sought out none other than John Sculley, CEO of Pepsi-Cola, in order to convince Sculley to leave his prominent position and run Steve's fledgling enterprise. Somehow, some way, Steve got the meeting. Sculley listened patiently to the young man's vision and, after several meetings, introduced the man sixteen years his junior to reality: "Well, you'd have to give me a million-dollar annual salary, a million-dollar signing bonus, and a million-dollar severance package."

Steve was taken by surprise; such figures were unthinkable. But his boldness had brought him this far, so he took a risk and said, "Okay, you've got it. Even if I have to pay for it out of my own pocket."

"Steve," Sculley replied, "I'd love to be an adviser to you, but I don't think I can come."

Steve's head dropped, then after a long pause, he issued a challenge that pierced Sculley to the depths of his being. Looking Sculley in the eye, Steve simply asked, "Do you want to spend the rest of your life selling sugared water, or do you want a chance to change the world?" And because of that challenge, Sculley resigned from Pepsi-Cola and became CEO of Steve's visionary little company. And the rest, as they say, is history. Young Steve was none other than Stephen Jobs, and his fledgling computer company was called Apple. Under Sculley's skillful leadership, Apple became one of the world's leaders in computer technology and pioneered the use of personal computers. Together, they really did change the world.[1]

That story has become legendary in business circles, not just because it chronicles the rise of a successful company, but because it speaks to our greatest fear and our greatest hope. Contrary to popular belief, I don't think that our greatest fear is death. We all know we're going to die, but none of us believe it will ever happen. No, when we quiet ourselves and reflect on what matters most, I think that our greatest fear is a wasted life. And our greatest hope? It's the opposite—a purposeful life.

The Academy Award-winning movie *Braveheart* told the story of the Scottish freedom fighter William Wallace. Toward the end of the film, Wallace is in chains, awaiting his execution. On the strength of his passion and determination, he had led all of Scotland to revolt against their English oppressors. Time and again, his will and determination had bonded the spirits of the people into a force for national identity, pride, and freedom. But now he had been betrayed, handed over to his enemies, and sentenced to death. In the scene, a young woman urges the imprisoned Wallace to do whatever he can—regardless of its impact on his life mission or personal convictions—to stay the hand of his enemies, in order that his life might be spared. His response communicates one of the deepest truths of human existence: "Every man dies," he said. "Not every man really lives."

And he was right.

Few of us devote our lives to great endeavors. We settle for selling sugared water instead of changing the world. We grow old and die, having never lived. Our worst and deepest fear becomes reality. But for many, the course they have traveled is not recognized until the end. An intriguing sociological study asked fifty people over the age of ninety-five one question: "If you could live your life over again, what would you do differently?"[2] These men and women had a unique perspective, looking back at the end of a very *long* life, rich with accumulated wisdom and insight. Three answers continually emerged and dominated the results of the study:

- If I had it to do over again, I would reflect more.

- If I had it to do over again, I would risk more.

- If I had it to do over again, I would do more things that would live on after I am dead.

But such regrets do not have to cloud life's closing moments.

Three Levels of Living

Many observers of the human condition have noted that we tend to live on one of three levels.[3] The first level is *survival*. For some, this survival is literal: They are poor and destitute, and they must spend every waking moment trying to make it through another day. Others may have full stomachs, but their survival mode is no less real. Their goal in life is simply to exist, to maintain, and to make it to another weekend. They live for the moment, exacting what pleasures or thrills they can in the face of a quickly passing life, which really isn't much of a life at all.

A second level of living, slightly higher up the ladder than survival, is *success*. Some people live to make it big—to get a big salary, a big car, and a big house. The problem, as you may have already discovered, is that when you get there, success doesn't really deliver the way you thought it would. It's not just that something bigger is always just beyond your reach, but that the deep sense of satisfaction you thought would come with material success *didn't*. In Arthur Miller's classic play *The Death of a Salesman*, the main character, Willie Loman, commits suicide after spending his entire life trying to be successful. His son stands by his father's grave and sadly concludes, "He had all the wrong dreams."

But fortunately, there is a third level of living that goes beyond survival and beyond success. This is the level of *significance*. Living a life of significance depends on finding and following your purpose. The Bible is full of people who discovered this truth. One example is David, who is widely considered among historians to be one of the greatest military and political leaders the world has ever produced. He is heralded for uniting the nation of Israel for one of its most glorious and influential eras. (He is also known for taking on a giant with very little ammunition.) But notice how the Bible depicts his greatness: "David . . . served God's purpose in his . . . generation" (Acts 13:36). The most significant thing the Bible could say about David was that he *found* and *followed* God's purpose for his life.

The essence of a significant life is catching a vision not only for what God is doing in this world, but for what He wants to do through you! The people who have the highest impact are not the most educated, the most wealthy, or even the most powerful. The people who make the biggest difference are those with the clearest sense of God's *purpose* for their lives. Why *is* that? Consider the following four reasons.

PURPOSE GIVES YOUR LIFE DIRECTION

The first reason that finding and following your God-given life purpose is so strategic is because it gives your life *direction*. We live in a world of seemingly endless choices and options. When John Naisbitt wrote his best-selling book *Megatrends* some years ago, he said that one of the top ten trends of the modern world is a shift from "no choice" to "multiple choice."[4] Seldom has a prediction been so quickly validated. You turn on the TV, and with cable, you have more than sixty channels to choose from. You go to the grocery store, only to find a hundred different breakfast cereals to choose from. I once heard that more than two hundred new grocery items come out *weekly*.

It reminds me of the foreign exchange student I heard about who came to America. He didn't know a great deal of English, so his language instructor told him, "Well, you have to eat, so let me tell you something basic to ask for in a restaurant. Just say, 'Hamburger, fries, Coke.'"

The student repeated, "Hamburger, fries, Coke."

"That's right," the instructor said. "Hamburger, fries, Coke."

So for three weeks, that's all he ate—hamburgers, fries, and Cokes. As you would imagine, he started to get pretty tired of his limited menu, so he went back to his teacher and said, "You've got to give me something else to say. I'm getting sick of eating hamburgers, fries, and Cokes all the time."

The teacher said, "Okay, but we still better keep it simple. You're just beginning to learn the language. Do you like breakfast food?"

"Sure," the student said. "I like breakfast."

"Okay, whenever you order at a restaurant, just say, 'Eggs, toast, juice.' That's it: 'Eggs, toast, juice.'"

The student could remember that, so the next day he went into a restaurant. When the waitress asked him for his order, he proudly said, "Eggs, toast, juice."

Without looking up from her pad, she asked, "Will that be scrambled eggs, fried eggs, boiled eggs, poached eggs, over easy, or eggs Benedict? And do you want white toast, rye, or wheat? And will it be orange juice, apple juice, grape juice, prune juice, or grapefruit juice?"

He looked up at her, paused a minute, and said, "Hamburger, fries, Coke."

You can feel his frustration, can't you? Life is full of endless decisions. What are you going to major in? Whom are you going to marry? Where are you going to work? How will you spend your time? What do you want to accomplish by the time you're seventy? The only way to have direction on these and many other issues is to have a clear sense of *purpose* for your life. And if your life has no purpose, you become frustrated, confused, and often overwhelmed. As the Bible notes, "A doubtful mind will be as unsettled as a wave of the sea that is driven and tossed by the wind; and every decision you then make will be uncertain, as you turn first this way, and then that" (James 1:6–8 TLB).

The need for finding and following your purpose in life is demonstrated in a thought-provoking scene in Lewis Carroll's classic children's tale *Alice's Adventures in Wonderland.* Young Alice comes to a fork in the road and asks the Cheshire Cat which direction she should take.

"That depends a good deal on where you want to get to," said the Cat.

"I don't much care where," said Alice.

"Then it doesn't matter which way you walk," said the Cat.[5]

And the Cat was right! If you have no sense of purpose, you can have little direction. Contrast this with the following promise of God: "For I know the plans I have for you. . . . They are plans for good and not for evil, to give you a future and a hope" (Jer. 29:11 TLB). God has plans for your life, and, if you

find and follow them, His plans will give you a future filled
with hope.

PURPOSE GIVES YOUR LIFE ENTHUSIASM

A second reason that a purposeful life is so important is that it gives
your life *enthusiasm*. The word *enthusiasm* comes from two Greek
words, *en* and *theos*. *Theos* is the Greek word for God, and *en* is like
our word *in,* so *enthusiasm* literally means "in God." An enthusiastic life is one that has God in it! God wants to do great things *in*
your life and *through* your life. He has a purpose for you, and finding and following His purpose gives you an energy, motivation, and
enthusiasm for living that you can't find any other way. This is what
Jesus had in mind when He said, "You're tied down to the mundane;
I'm in touch with what is beyond your horizons. You live in terms
of what you see and touch. I'm living on other terms. I told you that
you were missing God in all this. You're at a dead end. . . . You're
missing God in your lives" (John 8:23–24 MSG).

One biography of General William Booth, founder of the
Salvation Army, describes the moment when Booth's son,
Bramwell, informs his eighty-three-year-old father that a disease
within his eyes will result in blindness.

"You mean that I am blind?" the old man asks.

"Well, General," said his son, using one of the family's titles of
endearment. "I fear that we must contemplate that."

After a pause the old man said, "I shall never see your face
again?"

"No," his son answers. "Probably not in this world."

During the next few moments the veteran's hand crept along the counterpane to take hold of his son's, and holding it, he said very calmly, "God must know best!" And after another pause, "Bramwell, I have done what I could for God and for the people with my eyes. Now I shall do what I can for God and for the people without my eyes."[6] General Booth was able to have such an enthusiastic life because he had a life purpose rooted in God coursing through his veins.

Without purpose for their lives, people can lose their desire even to survive. During World War II, the Nazis had set up a camp factory in Hungary where prisoners were made to labor amid barbarous conditions. One day, the prisoners were ordered to move a huge pile of garbage from one end of the camp to the other. The next day, they were ordered to move the pile back to its original location. Thus began a pattern. Day after day, the prisoners were forced to haul the same mountain of garbage from one end of the camp to the other. Soon the impact on the prisoners of that mindless, meaningless labor and existence began to surface. An elderly prisoner began sobbing uncontrollably and had to be led away. Then another man began screaming until he was beaten into silence. A third man, who had endured three years of labor in the camp, suddenly broke away and began running toward the electrified fence. He was told to stop or he would be electricuted, but he didn't care. He flung himself on the fence and died in a blinding flash.

In the days that followed—moving the pile from one end of

the camp to the other—dozens of prisoners went insane, yet their captors were unfeeling. What the prisoners didn't know was that they were part of a Nazi experiment in mental health. The goal was to determine what would happen when people were subjected to meaningless activity. The Nazis wanted to see what life would become *without* a sense of purpose and concluded that the result was insanity and suicide. The commandant even remarked that at this rate, there would be no more need to use the gas chambers.[7]

PURPOSE GIVES YOUR LIFE FOCUS

So knowing your life purpose gives you much-needed direction, and it also gives you enthusiasm and motivation for living. But purpose also brings a third dynamic to bear on your life: *focus*. Without focus, our lives become filled with activity that results in very little significance. This meaningless activity is like the airplane that was flying coast to coast in the middle of the night. Two hours into the flight, the pilot's voice came over the intercom:

"Ladies and gentlemen, this is your captain speaking. We're flying at an altitude of thirty-seven thousand feet and at a speed of six hundred miles an hour.

"But I'm afraid," he continued, "that we have some good news and some bad news. The bad news is that our radar *and* our radio transmission have broken down, and we have absolutely no idea where we are."

After a pause, he added, "The good news is that wherever it is we're going, we're making excellent time!"

I find it interesting that when the apostle Paul talked about his life purpose, he said, "I am still not all I should be but I am bringing all my energies to bear on this one thing" (Phil. 3:13 TLB). In essence, Paul was saying that knowing his life purpose allowed him to bring focus to the activity of his life. More than just direction—which has to do with decisions—Paul's life had a specific focus, which had to do with how he was going to invest himself. Like all of us, Paul had limited time and energy. Knowing his purpose let him invest those resources strategically so that he made an impact with his life.

Think of how this works with light. The power of light depends almost entirely on focus. Light that is diffused doesn't make much of an impact. But if you put that light through a magnifying glass, it can set something on fire. If you concentrate that light even more, it becomes a laser that will cut through sheet metal. Just as light becomes more powerful as it is brought into focus, so our lives take on increasing levels of significance as we focus all of our energies on pursuing our life purposes.

PURPOSE GIVES YOUR LIFE COMMITMENT

On Wednesday, September 6, 1995, forty-two thousand people stood and cheered for one man—for more than twenty-two minutes! In fact, one writer said that all of America applauded. The person honored by their applause was baseball's Cal Ripken, Jr. who that night broke a record, set by the legendary Lou Gehrig, that had stood for decades. The record itself wasn't all that glamorous, playing in 2,131 consecutive games, but something about it touched our hearts because it was a record for *commitment*. When he didn't feel like playing, when the team was losing, or when the attendance was down, Ripkin still put on his uniform and, for fourteen seasons, faithfully trotted out to his position at shortstop. What breeds this kind of commitment? The same thing that gives direction, enthusiasm, and focus: *purpose*.

I've long been an admirer of former British prime minister Winston Churchill. One of the highlights of my visit to London was touring the underground Cabinet War Rooms where Churchill directed the British war effort during World War II. Faced with the Nazi war machine and the evil of Hitler, Churchill stood in front of the people of England and declared, "We shall go on to the end, we shall fight in France, we shall fight on the seas and oceans, we shall fight with growing confidence and strength in the air, we shall defend our island, whatever the cost may be, we shall fight on the beaches, we shall fight on the landing grounds, we shall fight in the fields and in the streets, we shall fight in the hills; we shall never surrender."[8]

And they didn't. However, another war was not able to generate such rhetoric, much less result. The Vietnam War was met with campus demonstrations, protest marches, burning of draft registration cards, and angry denunciations through poetry and music. Why? The answers have filled countless books and articles, but the overwhelming mantra of the day was that *there didn't seem to be a purpose to the war.*

The challenges of life cannot be met without a clear sense of purpose; for without purpose, there is no commitment. This is the spirit behind the apostle Paul's admonition in 1 Corinthians 15:58 to remain steadfast and immovable in regard to the challenges and tasks of life, because our lives are about the work God has given us to pursue.

New Beginnings

One of the more thoughtful movies to come out in the last few years was *City Slickers,* which exposed the midlife crises of three men who were in search of themselves and their places in life. In one scene, the character played by Billy Crystal, Mitch, asks his boss, "Have you ever reached a point in your life where you say to yourself, 'This is the best I'm ever gonna look, this is the best I'm ever gonna feel, this is the best I'm ever gonna do,' and it ain't that great?" Later in the movie, another character makes a similarly somber assessment, saying, "At this point in life, where you are is where you are."

Not true. You may not have become the rock star you dreamed of or the superstar athlete you mimicked on the basketball court, but you can fulfill *your* purpose for *your* life and for *your* time. God is ready to go. New beginnings are His specialty, and taking human beings and filling them with a deep sense of His unique purpose for their lives is His passion. The Bible says, "God has made us what we are, and in our union with Christ Jesus he has created us for a life of good deeds, which he has already prepared for us to do" (Eph. 2:10 TEV). The question is whether *we* are prepared to live the life He offers.

A DAY AT DISNEY

Some years ago, on a Sunday afternoon, a father took his eight-year-old son to Disneyland. As they stood on the bridge that spans the moat around the Fantasyland Castle, the little boy said, "Dad, I want to talk to the wisest man in the world." Apparently the boy had learned about Solomon at Sunday school that morning, and he wanted what Solomon had gained through his wisdom—namely, riches, power, and fame.

The father laughingly said, "Well, that isn't me, son." Another man was standing nearby, watching and listening to the exchange with a pleasant expression on his face. Not knowing what else to say to his son, the father jokingly pointed to the nearby man and said, "Maybe *he's* the wisest man in the world. Why don't you ask him?" Surprisingly, the boy did!

As his father watched, the boy shyly approached the man and said, "Sir, my father says you might be the wisest man in the world."

The man smiled at the boy. "I'm not the wisest man in the world," he said, "but perhaps I can be of help. I will give you four words.

"First," the man said, "is *think*. Think about the principles you are going to live by. Principles are rules that will guide you through

14

life. What you believe is important. You will need your principles to guide you on your journey through life.

"The second word," the man continued, "is *dream*. Dream a big dream in which you play a starring role. What do you intend to do when you grow up? What is it that you'll love doing, the thing that God gave you the talent to do very, very well? That gift becomes the music you were meant to make. It adds a magnificent purpose to your life. Dream a *big* dream!

"The third word," he said, "is *believe*. Believe that you are as special as your mom and dad and God all know you to be. Believe in your principles and your dreams.

"And the final word," the man said, "is *dare*. Dare to develop your dream, your special vision for a good, useful, and great life, a life that will make a difference. Dare to make it happen. Dare to live your dream. And when you are wise, you'll know that there are many kinds of riches that are far more valuable than money, gold, or jewels."

The young boy listened intently. "Thank you, sir," the boy said. "I will remember your four words." Then, almost as an after-thought, he asked, "Will you tell me your name so I can tell my dad who you are?"

The man smiled and said, "My name is Walter Elias Disney."[9]

These are good words from a man who actually *followed* them. But we can *all* follow his advice. And it begins with discovering what it means to be human.

CHAPTER TWO

What It Means to Be Human

In the children's book *Is a Blue Whale the Biggest Thing There Is?*, you learn that the largest animal on earth is the blue whale. Its flippers alone are bigger than most animals on earth.[1] But as you turn the pages, you learn that the blue whale isn't anywhere *near* as big as a mountain. If you put one hundred blue whales in a huge jar, you could put millions of whale jars inside a hollowed-out Mt. Everest. But Mt. Everest isn't anywhere *near* as big as the earth. One hundred Mount Everests stacked on top of one another would be just a whisker on the face of the earth.

And the earth isn't anywhere *near* as big as the sun. You could fit one million earths inside the sun. But the sun, which is really just a medium-sized star, isn't anywhere *near* as big as a red supergiant star like Antares. But Antares isn't anywhere *near* as big as the Milky Way galaxy. Billions of stars, including supergiants like Antares, as well as countless comets and asteroids, make up the Milky Way galaxy. The size of the average galaxy is about six hundred trillion miles, and the average distance from one galaxy to another is twenty million trillion miles. To avoid awkwardly large numbers, astronomers speak in terms of light years, which is the distance that light travels in one year at a speed of 186,000 miles per second. So a light year is about six trillion miles. In those terms, the size of a galaxy is one hundred thousand light years, and the average distance between galaxies is roughly three million light years. But the Milky Way galaxy isn't anywhere *near* as big as the universe. There are *billions* of other galaxies in the universe. And yet, filled with billions of galaxies, the universe is almost totally empty. The distances from one galaxy to another are beyond our imagination.[2]

So who *are* we in the midst of this awesome cosmic order?

The question reminds me of a bizarre event that followed World War II. More than two hundred Frenchmen returned to Paris suffering from amnesia. They had gone through a horrible ordeal in Japanese prison camps that included extended solitary confinement and relentless torture. These men had been so psychologically traumatized that they had lost the conscious awareness of who they were.

In most of the cases, French officials were able to identify the men through Red Cross records or through the help of fellow prisoners. Yet of the two hundred men, thirty-two remained who could not be identified. So they published the photographs of those men on the front page of newspapers throughout the country, announcing a day and a time for anyone who had information on these men to come to the Paris Opera House. On that day, a large number of people filed in to the famed theater and took their seats. One by one, the amnesia victims walked onto the darkened stage, stood in the spotlight, and with heartbreaking hope in their voices, asked, "Does anybody out there know who I am?"[3]

But even with our memory intact, many of us are asking the same question. Just who and what *are* we? What does it mean to be human? What separates us from the rest of life? The Bible gives an intriguing answer: "Then God said, 'Let us make man in our image, in our likeness, and let them rule over the fish of the sea and the birds of the air, over the livestock, over all the earth, and over all the creatures that move along the ground.' So God created man in his own image, in the image of God he created him; male and female he created them" (Gen. 1:26–27).

In those verses, we find four amazing statements about who we are.

WE WERE MADE

The Bible begins by saying that we were created, *personally*, by God. This idea is becoming increasingly fashionable in the most unlikely of places, the world of secular science. One-time Plumian Professor of Astrophysics at Cambridge University Sir Fred Hoyle, has determined that if you compute the time required to get all two hundred thousand amino acids for one human cell to come together by chance, it would be about 293.5 times the estimated age of the earth, which is usually set at around 4.6 billion years.[4] This would be akin to having the software for the latest Windows application result, *by chance*, from an explosion in a computer warehouse. Physicist Stephen Hawking once told a reporter, "The odds against a universe like ours emerging out of something like the big bang are enormous. . . . I think clearly there are religious implications."[5] Going even further, Hawking conceded that "it would be very difficult to explain why the universe should have begun in just this way, except as the act of a God who intended to create beings like us."[6]

This has led to what some have called the anthropic principle, which states that our world is uniquely suited to human beings and the rise of carbon-based life. In a National Public Radio interview, Owen Gingerich, professor of astronomy and the history of science at the Harvard-Smithsonian Center for Astrophysics in Cambridge, remarked, "There are so many wonderful details which, if they were changed only slightly, would make it impossible for us to be here, that one just has to feel, somehow, that there is a design in the universe and, therefore, a designer to have worked it out so magnificently."[7] Or as theoretical physicist Paul Davies of Cambridge has observed, "We are meant to be here."[8]

Our lives are *not* the result of chance. We didn't come from nothingness. To think otherwise would strip human life of any meaning. Unfortunately, this was the view of playwright Samuel Beckett, who put forth a play titled *Breath*. The curtain opened to a bare stage littered with nothing but garbage—no actors, no dialogue. The script was nothing but a soundtrack, only thirty seconds in length, beginning with a baby's first cry and ending with an old man's last, dying gasp. Then the curtain closed. Beckett's point was clear: Life is absurd, man is meaningless, and existence is pointless. We come from nothing and go to nothing. Sören Kierkegaard compares such views to a smooth, flat stone that is thrown over the surface of a pond. The stone dances and skims over the surface of the water until that moment comes when, like life without hope or meaning, it runs out of momentum and sinks into nothingness.[9]

So the worldview of the Bible is profound. If we are made by a designer, then we are not here by chance. Life is not a series of random developments. We were created for a reason. There is intentionality about each and every one of us. We are not accidents. *We were meant to be.*

I once heard a speaker remind his audience of this truth in a very *earthy* way. He said, "Did you ever consider that you were once a sperm? One of *five million* sperm? And you and these five million other sperm all lined up at this starting line. And at the end was *one egg.* And you all raced to get there—*and you won!* Compared to the Olympics, what you have pulled off is incredible! The odds were *five million to one,* and you came through! Don't let anybody tell you you're a loser. You wouldn't *be* here if you weren't a winner!" After the laughter died down, the point sank in. He was *right.* Against incredible biological odds, God willed each of us into existence, marking our lives full of purpose and meaning.

It took a while for a young girl by the name of Heather to discover this truth. At the age of eighteen months, she contracted a fever after her DPT shots. Hospitalized and near death, the medication given to her caused profound, lifelong hearing loss. Over the years, she was torn between whether to live as a hearing-impaired person in a hearing world or to stay within the safer confines of the nonhearing world. Over and over she prayed, "God, who am I? Hearing or deaf?" She sank to the lowest level of her life. The future seemed bleak and hopeless, the past nothing but a wasted effort.

Then Heather started to read the Bible. One day, she came to the story of Thomas, the disciple who doubted the resurrection of Jesus. As she read John 20:29, "Blessed are those who have not seen and yet have believed," she realized that no one can see or hear God. Just like her, a hearing-impaired person, everyone else must know God with their hearts, not their senses. Suddenly, Heather realized she was just like everyone else, someone whom God had made and loved. "Though I still didn't know where I'd find a place in this world, I knew that I was in capable hands—God's." Resting in her newly discovered identity, her place in the world began to unfold. On September 17, 1994, Heather Whitestone was crowned Miss America, the first physically disabled Miss America in the pageant's history, giving her a worldwide platform for championing the needs of the hearing impaired, as well as the cause of Christ.[10]

IN THE IMAGE OF GOD

Not only were we made by God, but the Bible tells us that we were made *in the image* of God. In other words, when God made us, He put something of Himself in us. He gave us a spark of the eternal, a portion of the divine. The image of God is more than just intelligence, consciousness, or the ability to think and reason. Being made in the image of God means that we each have a *soul*. And that soul is what allows us to do what only humans can do: be in a relationship with God.

This is decisive to who and what we are. We are made in the image of God, and God is community; He *is* relationship. In Genesis 1:26, the Bible uses the term "us" for God. This is one of many references in the Bible to the triune nature of God, that God is trinity, three in one: God the Father, God the Son, and God the Holy Spirit. God is a community of three persons in one being. He is not three gods, but three persons who *are* one God. And because God is Himself a community of oneness, He created us to be in community with each other and, most importantly, with Him.

So being made in the image of God is profound, and it is unique to human beings. Nothing else in all of creation as we know it bears the image of God—not plants, animals, reptiles, insects, fish, nor birds. And bearing the image of God means that we have the ability—and responsibility—to respond and relate to God. God is relational, and He wants us to be in a relationship with Him. We were made to be in community with our Creator!

But just knowing that we are made in the image of God is not enough. We must grasp its *significance*. So before we move on, let me just throw out two reasons why bearing the image of God is so notable: First, if the Bible is true, then you cannot be who you were made to be *apart* from a relationship with God. As Os Guinness has written, our primary calling is not to somewhere, or something, but to Someone.[11] If being human means that you were made *by* God, in the *image* of God, for *relationship* with God, then you will never experience full humanity until you are *in* that relationship. C. S. Lewis likened this to the idea of a lifeless, toy tin soldier coming "fully and splendidly alive."[12]

Searching for purpose apart from a relationship with God is like searching for answers where there are none. Munich comedian Karl Vallentin was famous for a skit that illustrates this folly. Coming onto the stage in almost total darkness, with one solitary circle of light provided by a street lamp, he paces round and round with a long, worried face, searching for something. Soon a policeman crosses the stage and asks him what he has lost. Vallentin answers that it is the key to his house. The policeman joins in the hunt, but after a while the search appears to be fruitless.

"Are you sure you lost it here?" asks the policeman.

"Oh no!" says Vallentin, pointing to a dark corner. "It was over there."

"Then why on earth are you looking here?" asks the policeman.

"There's no light over there!" replies Vallentin.[13]

A second significance of bearing the image of God is that every human being—*every single one*—has value. No matter what a person's skin color, income, ethnicity, or mental or physical capability, every human being has incalculable value and significance. You may be reading this book, feeling that your life doesn't count for much, that you aren't important, or that you don't matter to God. You couldn't be more wrong. The fact that you were created in the image of God gives you *infinite* worth.

Mary Ann Bird tells of growing up knowing she was different and hating it. She was born with a cleft palate, and when she started school, her classmates made it clear they saw her as a little girl with a misshapen lip, crooked nose, lopsided teeth, and garbled speech. When they would ask her what happened to her lip, she would lie and say that she had fallen and cut it on a piece of glass. Somehow it seemed more acceptable to have suffered an accident than to have been born different. She grew up convinced that no one outside of her family could ever love her. Then she entered the second grade and had a teacher named Mrs. Leonard. Everyone loved Mrs. Leonard. She was short, round, and always happy. People even said that she sparkled.

Every year the school gave all of the students a hearing test. One day Mrs. Leonard said it was time for that year's test, and she began to administer it to every student in the class. Finally, it was Mary Ann's turn. She knew from past years that as she stood against the door and covered one ear, the teacher sitting at her desk would whisper something, and then she would have to whisper it back—sentences like "The sky is blue" or "Do you have new shoes?" But when it was her turn, Mrs. Leonard said seven words that forever changed Mary Ann's life.

Her teacher whispered, "I wish you were my little girl."[14]

And that's what God says to each one of us, no matter how we feel about ourselves, even if we have wandered far from Him, even in the midst of our sin and failure and weakness. He says, "I made you because I wanted to be in a relationship with you. I love you. I want you to be My child."

WITH SINGULAR UNIQUENESS

But that's not all: The Bible makes a third statement about who we are. Not only are human beings created by God and in the image of God, but God made us *male* and *female*. When God created human beings, He intentionally created diversity. He deliberately made us a race of men and a race of women. This also helps us understand who we are, because the differences aren't just biological. Men and women are different relationally, emotionally, and psychologically. As John Gray has written, sometimes the differences are so profound that it's as if men are from Mars, and women are from Venus![15]

One day, my wife, Susan, and I were exploring a bookstore, and she excitedly said, "Jim! You have to see this book I found! It's just great!" So I went over to where she had been looking and saw her pointing out a book titled *What Men Know About Women*. I opened the book, and guess what I read? Nothing! Every single page in *What Men Know About Women* was blank. Now I'm somewhat slow, so I thought it was a misprint. So I reached up and got another copy off the shelf, leafed through it, and found that it didn't have anything written in it either. Then I got it. I looked over at my wife, and she was dying with laughter. She loved it!

But it's true, isn't it? Men don't know much about women. And women don't know much about us men either. The differences between men and women are good to remember because of their broader implications. Not everyone thinks alike, feels alike, or reacts alike. Even further, each of us is individually unique, even beyond our gender. God made us all humans—in His image, as men and women—but He then gave each and every one of us utterly unique characteristics. Every human being that has ever been born is one of a kind, including *you*.

Play a game with me. Let's hum together. (Come on . . . you know you've always wanted to hum while reading a book!)

Here we go. "Hmmmmmmmmmmmmmm."

You didn't do it, did you? Come on, just a short one. Nobody's listening.

"Hmmmmmmmmmmmmm."

You know what you heard? The only hum with that tone in the world. That's right, none of us has the same pitch. There's a difference between every human voice. *No* one in the world has *your* voice.

Now take a look at your fingers. You have probably heard that no one who has ever lived, or ever will live, has your fingerprints. Even the retina of your eye is unique. But your individuality is not just in regard to your physical makeup. You are unique in terms of your personality, passions, giftedness, and abilities.

You are the only *you* who ever will be.

FOR A PURPOSE

So as a human being, you were created by God in the image of God with a singular uniqueness. This leads us to the Bible's fourth declaration about who we are: people with a *purpose*. Look again at what the Bible says: "'Let them [human beings] rule over the fish of the sea and the birds of the air, over the live-stock, over all the earth, and over all the creatures that move along the ground'" (Gen. 1:26).

Only humans were given responsibilities of oversight. God told us to fill the earth, to subdue it, to multiply, and to rule. Initially, this was a word to the responsibility we have as the stewards of this planet. Issues such as the extinction of animals, the ruination of rain forests, and the erosion of the ozone layer are important, not just because our lives might depend on it, but because God has given us the responsibility for managing, caring for, and cultivating the earth.

But the significance of this responsibility goes even deeper. The Bible is saying that to be human means to have a purpose in life. Ours was not meant to be a meaningless existence. God doesn't make anything without a clear, driving purpose—and that includes each and every human being. God has a purpose for your life. He has created you for a reason. One writer has noted that there are more than one thousand references in the Old and New Testaments that tell us that God has a plan and a purpose for our lives.[16] Not only does God have a fundamental call on every human life to live as He intended and to become all that He dreams, but He also has a specific purpose for your life as it relates to your vocation, activities, investments, and mission. Before he won the Nobel Prize for literature, Alexander Solzhenitsyn faced death through cancer. Upon his recovery, he realized that "all the life given back to me [is not] mine in the full sense: it is built around a purpose."[17] Every event and activity in your life is infused with significance.

There was once a traveler who came from Italy to the French town of Chartres to see the great church that was being built there. Arriving at the end of the day, he went to the site just as the workmen were leaving for home. He asked one man, covered with dust, what he did at the work site. The man replied that he was a stonemason; he spent his days carving rocks. Another man, when asked, said that he was a glassblower who spent his days making slabs of colored glass. Still another workman replied that he was a blacksmith who pounded iron for a living. Wandering into the church, the traveler came upon an elderly woman, armed only with a broom, who was sweeping up the chips and shavings from the day's work.

"What are you doing?" he asked.

The woman paused, leaned on her broom. Looking up toward the high arches, she replied, "Me? I'm building a cathedral for the glory of the Almighty God."[18]

So are we all.

Ben the Bastard Boy

Fred Craddock taught preaching for years at the Candler School of Theology at Emory University, outside of Atlanta. He once described the time he went to a small restaurant in Gatlinburg, Tennessee.[19] An old man walked in, stood by his table, and asked, "What's your name?"

Craddock was trying to have a nice, quiet visit with his wife, and he didn't feel like having an additional conversation with anyone, much less a strange old man. So he answered rather abruptly,

"Fred," and then turned back to his wife, hoping the old guy got the hint.

But the man pressed on, asking, "What do you do, Fred?"

Craddock searched for an answer that would encourage his newfound friend to go away. To quickly end the conversation, he replied, "I'm a professor of homiletics at a theological seminary." The old guy just looked at him and said, "You're a preacher!" Then he pulled up a chair and sat down. "I've got a preacher story. Mind if I join you?"

Fred gave up. "Please, be our guest."

The man pointed out the window. "Mister, you see those hills? I was born back there in those hills. And when I was born they called me 'Ben the Bastard Boy,' because that's what I was, a bastard. I didn't know who my father was.

"And when I'd walk down the street I'd have the feeling that everyone was looking at me, saying, 'There goes Ben the Bastard boy, I wonder who his father is. . . . I wonder who his father is.' And when I'd walk, I'd always walk with my head down because I was a bastard. When I was in school I would always sit in the back of the room. When the other kids would go out to play, I would stay inside because I was Ben the Bastard Boy.

"When I was twelve, we got a new preacher in town, and everybody talked about how good he was. I'd never been to church before, but I went to church because the talk on this minister was so good. I heard him preach, and they were right—he was good. But I always went late and left early because I didn't want to talk to anybody coming or going. Then one Sunday the preacher was so good that I forgot to leave! Before I realized it, the service was over. People were squeezed into the aisles, and I couldn't get out. And then I felt a heavy hand on my shoulder. I turned around and saw that big preacher-man looking down on me. He said, 'Boy,' and I just turned and said, 'Yeah?' He said, 'Boy, what's your name?' Without waiting for an answer, he said, 'Who's your father, boy? What's your father's name?'

"And when he asked me that, it was like he put a knife in my stomach. The pain shot from the bottom of my toes to the top of my head. I just felt pain and agony. But he wasn't finished. He said, 'Boy, I know who your father is. I know his name.' And I looked up and wondered whether he *did* know!

"Then that preacher-man said, 'Boy, your father is God. You are a child of God. Don't you ever forget that you are a child of God, you understand me? That's who you are.'"

Then the old man, moved by the telling of his own story, wiped away a few tears and asked to be excused. But as he got up, he said, "Mister, that simple statement, 'Your father is God. You are a child of God,' changed my whole life."

And then he walked out the door. Craddock and his wife sat in silence, stunned by the old man's tale. Then their waitress hurried over and asked, "Do you know whom you were talking to?"

Fred shrugged, "Just an old man named Ben."

"That was Ben Hooper," she gasped, "the governor of Tennessee!"

Ben Hooper knew who he was, and it changed his life. It can change yours too.

CHAPTER THREE

Examining the Call of God

A young girl named Martha attended a large public school outside of Indianapolis. She was shy and didn't have very many friends. She had the unfortunate distinction of reaching her senior year in high school without ever having a date. During the fall of her senior year, a very popular girl named Julie was assigned as her lab partner in chemistry. Julie invited Martha to a Halloween party. It was Martha's first invitation to a party since she was eight years old.

Understandably nervous and scared, she walked through the door of Julie's home, tried to say hello to the few people she knew, and stood on the edges of the groups of people, listening in on the conversations. In one corner of the living room was a group of boys. They would look around the room, talk in low voices, and then burst out laughing. Suddenly, Martha realized they were all looking at her. Then they laughed louder than ever. Martha didn't know what to do but turn away and try to hide.

Later in the evening, a boy she hardly knew sat down near her, and she remembered that he had been part of the group that was laughing. Gathering up her courage, she asked him what it had been about. After an awkward silence, the boy told her that they had been playing a game where they looked at people and tried to say which animal they look like. He told her that Julie, the popular girl, was easy: She was a deer. Mark was a giraffe. Cheryl was a chipmunk.

"What about me?" nervously ventured Martha. "You did me. I saw you."

"Sure," the boy answered. "You were a dog."

Then he started laughing all over again. When Martha went home that night and looked in the mirror, that's what she saw—a dog. For years, whenever a boy would look at her, that's what she felt in her heart that he saw. And for years, whenever she looked at herself, the words came to her over and over: "You're a dog."[1]

What's running through your heart and mind when it comes to who you think you are? Is it a crippling, defeating echo of words that binds you to a sense of failure and insecurity? It shouldn't be, no matter what lies in your past. When you look in the mirror, the only words that matter are the words of God, and those words reveal a fundamental calling on your life that forms the foundation of your life purpose. Martha was not a dog, and neither are you. Believe it or not, God's call on your life begins with your call to be a saint.[2]

SAINTS

What comes to your mind when you hear the word *saint?* Many of us think of someone like Mother Teresa, someone who has taken an oath of poverty and endured endless hardships, someone who is fairly old, stooped over, and living in unspeakable conditions in order to try to honor God. So when we come across the idea that one of the foundational purposes of every life is to be a saint, we are taken aback. Why? Because none of us see ourselves as being very saintly.

Yet if you are in a relationship with God through Christ, God has declared you to be a saint. When Paul wrote to the church at Ephesus, he addressed his letter "to the *saints* in Ephesus" (Eph. 1:1; emphasis added). So what is sainthood all about? How can you ever fulfill this purpose in life? You may have come from a background that considers saints to be figures from history that the church recognizes as people to be venerated, even prayed to. Well, while it's good to respect and honor the lives of people who have committed themselves to God, the Bible doesn't know anything about a special class of people like that. So relax. Help is found in the word itself; *saint* means "someone who is set apart." The moment you trust Christ—confessing your sin, turning from it, and then coming to Christ as both leader and forgiver—something dramatic happens to your spiritual position. You are a new creation—a *saint*—in the eyes of God.

I read of a Christian professor who was teaching a sociology class at the University of Pennsylvania. Being a Christian in a secular university, he tried to work in an appropriate word about Jesus. He said, "Have you ever thought about what the various leaders of the world throughout history would have said to a prostitute?"

The class didn't quite know how to respond, so he prompted

them. "Come on, think with me. What would some of the world's leaders and philosophers have said to a prostitute? How about Buddha?" Nobody knew. "Mohammed?" Silence. "Moses?" Blank stares.

Then, sensing his moment, he asked, "How many of you have ever wondered what Jesus would have said to a prostitute?" Then a student on the front row, who was an atheist, said, "He never met one."

And the Christian professor thought to himself, *Aha!* He said, "Not so! Let me show you where in the New Testament Jesus met a prostitute." And just as he was about to "whip out the Word" on this guy, the student said, "Doctor, you didn't hear what I said. Jesus never met a prostitute!" The professor answered, "I say that He did, and I'm gonna show you where the story is in the Bible."

Then the student said, "Sir, when he met Mary Magdalene, do you think he saw a prostitute?" The professor was dumbfounded with the student's insight. He didn't mind having his theology corrected, but it was a little humiliating for it to be done by an atheist. Though he wasn't a Christian, his student had a better grasp of Christianity. He was absolutely right: Jesus never met a prostitute. He didn't look at people that way.[3]

But our sainthood is not simply a declaration by God that has nothing to do with our daily lives. One of our chief purposes is to *cooperate* with God's efforts to develop us into saints *functionally*. When you become a Christian, God has a very clear agenda for your life: to make you like Jesus. He wants to transform you into the person He has declared you to be. One of the most remarkable verses in the Bible is found in the Book of Ezekiel, where God says: "I will give you a new heart and put a new spirit in you; I will remove from you your heart of stone and give you a heart of flesh" (Ezek. 36:26). As C. S. Lewis explains it:

> Imagine yourself as a living house. God comes in to rebuild that house. At first, perhaps, you can understand what He is doing. He is getting the drains right and stopping the leaks in the rooms and so on: you knew that those jobs needed doing and so you are not surprised. But presently He starts knocking the house about in a way that hurts abominably and does not seem to make sense. What on earth is He up to? The explanation is that He is building quite a different house from the one you thought of—throwing out a new wing here, putting on an extra floor there, running up towers, making courtyards. You thought you were going to be made into a decent little cottage: but He is building a palace. He intends to come and live in it Himself.[4]

It's as if God says, "You are a saint—now live like one!" And the good news is that this purpose is not a pipe dream. As a Christian, you *can* begin developing into the saint that God has declared you to be through His power and presence.[5]

An old legend from the sheep country of England tells of two men who were arrested and convicted for stealing sheep. The magistrate sent them to prison for several years and decreed that the letter *S* be burned into their foreheads with a hot iron so that no one would ever forget their crimes. When the jail terms ended, one of the men left the area and was never heard from again. The other man repented of his crimes and dedicated his life to God. He determined to remain in the community in order to reconcile himself with the people and to serve their needs.

As the years passed, everyone fell into the second man's debt because of the way he freely gave of himself to care for them in their sicknesses, family crises, and work difficulties. Eventually, no one remembered or even spoke of his earlier crime of sheep stealing; they talked only of all that he had given them out of a heart of grace and love. One day two small boys saw the now-elderly man pass by. They asked their mother why he had an *S* on his forehead. The mother told them she didn't know, but if she had to guess, the mark stood for "saint."[6]

SOLDIER

General Fred Franks fought in the Vietnam War. While on the battlefield, a grenade known as a "potato masher" exploded near Franks, and he lost his leg. After months of recuperation and physical therapy, Franks remained as an amputee in the army, eventually rising to the position of lieutenant general commander of the VII Corps. This proved to be the greatest challenge of his military life because, under his command, the VII Corps provided the main coalition force that broke the back of Iraq's Republican Guard in Desert Storm, considered the greatest American military triumph since World War II.[7]

Fred Franks is, by anyone's standards, a soldier. And not many of us would ever think of placing ourselves alongside his life. We wear white shirts and ties, not fatigues. We drive vans and SUVs, not Bradley tanks. We step outside and smell smoke from our backyard grills, not from artillery fire. The noise overhead comes from U.S. Airways, not the U.S. Air Force. Fred Franks may be a soldier, but most of us are not.

Yet being a soldier is one of the foundational purposes of our lives.

Let's look again at the Book of Ephesians, where we find one of the most provocative and stirring passages in all the Bible: "Be strong in the Lord and in his mighty power. Put on the full armor of God so that you can take your stand against the devil's schemes. For our struggle is not against flesh and blood, but against the rulers, against the authorities, against the powers of this dark world and against the spiritual forces of evil in the heavenly realms" (Eph. 6:10–12).

The Bible teaches that a spiritual battle is taking place between good and evil in the heavenly realms, a powerful conflict between God and the spiritual forces arrayed against Him, led by the evil one, Satan. Jesus believed in Satan; He didn't think the devil was a myth or a figment of someone's imagination. Jesus taught that we need to take Satan seriously, because Satan has declared all-out war against God.

This is a real conflict—not against flesh and blood, but against the great spiritual forces that war against God in heaven. As Eugene Peterson has paraphrased the apostle Paul's words, "This is no afternoon athletic contest that we'll walk away from and forget about in a couple of hours. This is for keeps, a life-or-death fight to the finish against the Devil and all his angels" (Eph. 6:12–13 MSG). That's the battle. And it's raging with fury beyond our understanding.

God wants you to be a soldier in that spiritual war. He wants you in His army. There's a war going on between good and evil, and He wants you to be part of the fight—on the front lines, as a player, making a difference. The call of God isn't to be a bench sitter, a passive spectator, or an apathetic bystander. He wants you to bring everything you have—gifts, abilities, resources, strengths, position, determination, and will—to the fray.

In the summer of 1978, I worked in Colorado on a project for one of my father's companies. One weekend, I took some time off and visited the city of Fort Collins. I went to see a movie that had just been released. It was the second installment of the *Star Wars* trilogy, *The Empire Strikes Back*.

As you know, the *Star Wars* saga is about the cosmic battle between good and evil, specifically, of a young farm boy named Luke Skywalker, who became swept up in the galactic rebellion against the evil empire. Now this may sound a bit off base to you, but watching *The Empire Strikes Back* was a very defining moment for me. When I walked out of the movie, I was struck to the depth of my soul. I remember sitting in my car in the theater parking lot, thinking, *That's what I want out of life: to be caught up in the sweep of history. To be in the center of things. To be making a difference. To be at the heart of the struggle between good and evil.*

My heart was almost breaking at the thought of a life of insignificance. Then I remember thinking, *Where can that happen in the real world? How can I be a part of something that is bigger than myself?* And it struck me: That's what God's invitation to the Christian life is all about: the cosmic battle between good and evil. There *was* a galactic struggle going on, and I *could* be a player. It became crystal clear to me that I could give my life to something that would live on after I was gone, something that was bigger than I was, something that would impact all of history, even into eternity. The reality of the spiritual realm, the spiritual struggle for people's souls, and the eternal consequences at stake—I could give my life to *that!* What I didn't realize is that being in God's army was already the call on my life. *And it's also the call on yours.*

AMBASSADOR

The president of the United States has the power and responsibility to appoint ambassadors to represent the United States to nations throughout the world. Being an ambassador is quite an honor. Usually, an appointment to be an ambassador only comes at the end of a long and distinguished career. The candidate must be educated, polished, and relationally gifted. His communication skills should be of the highest caliber, and his negotiation abilities must be readily available. Ambassadors need to be effective hosts, diplomats, confidants, and sometimes, even spies. They must be cool-headed in a crisis and able to exercise sensitive and strong leadership skills during times of unrest.

The many qualifications of being an ambassador can be rather intimidating. So when we hear that one of the foundational purposes of our lives is to be an ambassador—for *God,* no less—it's understandable that we do a bit of a double take. Many of us feel unqualified, intimidated, overwhelmed, and just plain nervous about being God's ambassadors. Yet the Bible is clear:

> If anyone is in Christ, he is a new creation; the old has gone, the new has come! All this is from God, who reconciled us to himself through Christ and gave us the ministry of reconciliation: that God was reconciling the world to himself in Christ, not counting men's sins against them. And he has committed to us the message of reconciliation. We are therefore Christ's ambassadors, as though God were making his appeal through us. (2 Cor. 5:17–20)

The word *reconciled* means "reunited, brought together, healed, restored to who we were meant to be." When we come to God through faith in Jesus Christ, He appoints us as His ambassadors, and He wants to tell the world about His reconciling message of love and hope and healing *through us.*

Now, if you're like me, when I first heard that, I thought, *God's in trouble, because I'm no ambassador, and I don't want to become one either.* The first thing that entered my mind was having to hand out tracts on a street corner or be obnoxious and pushy with people at work. But that is not God's call on our lives. He does not call us to be pushy, obnoxious, intolerant, or arrogant. So how do we fulfill our life purpose as an ambassador? God simply wants us to be willing to invest in other people *relationally,* seeing every life as a life of value and then reaching out in care and concern.

I read about a first grader named Tommy who had a friend at school named Jay. Jay lived on a farm, and his father died in a tractor accident. Tommy prayed for his friend every day. One day, he saw Jay walking down the stairs at school and decided to reach out to him.

"Hey, Jay, how are you getting along?" Tommy asked.

"Oh, fine, just fine," Jay said.

"You know," Tommy ventured, "I've been praying for you ever since your daddy was killed."

Then Jay stopped, grabbed Tommy's hand, and led him out behind the school building. When they got there, he said, "You know, that was a lie when I said things are going fine. They aren't going fine. We are having trouble with the cows and with the machines. My mother doesn't know what to do. But I didn't know you were praying for me."[8]

Ambassadors reach out with the care and concern of Christ. They share the life-changing message about the love of God and His desire to forgive people of their sins and to lead them in their lives. Ambassadors are willing and able to talk about Who God is and what He has done in their lives, and through that, cast a vision to others about what He can do in *their* lives. Michael Green once made the observation that the early church were some of the world's best ambassadors. His observation about what made them so effective is telling: They shared the gospel like it was gossip over the backyard fence.[9]

Let's say you were diagnosed with a rare form of cancer. There was no known cure, and you were given less than a year to live. Then a new, experimental drug came on the market, and you gave it a try. Within three months, your disease was completely cured. The following year, a friend of yours is diagnosed with the same disease. Would you even *think* about not sharing your experience with your friend? Would it even enter your mind *not* to let him or her know about the cure? Of course not! Sharing your experience would be the most natural thing in the world to do because you know it could save your friend's life.

When my oldest daughter, Rebecca, was ten years old, we had a conversation that took a surprising turn: After discussing such things as tennis and school, she asked me *why* some people don't go to church. I answered her questions as honestly and frankly as I knew how. We talked about all of the reasons why people reject the church or turn away from Christ and what the implications of that decision would be for their lives. I didn't say a word about what that should mean to her as a Christian, but I could see her little heart just welling up with concern for those people. She sat for a minute, and then she looked up and said, "Daddy, I sure do hope that there are some girls in my tennis class who don't go to church so that I can invite them to come."

That is what being an ambassador is all about. You are called to be God's ambassador, and so am I. It's an incredible calling. Take the risk and extend an invitation to a friend to attend church or explore the faith, see him or her respond, and then watch your friend come up and say, "Thanks." Your heart will just about burst. You'll say, "God, look who I am! Look what I'm doing! Look at the difference it made in my friend's life, and I got to play a part! God, this is great!"

And God will whisper in your heart, *Want to do it again?* And you'll say, "Do it again? I want to be doing this the rest of my life!" And God will say, *Good, because that's who I made you to be: My ambassador to the world.*

FRIEND

I grew up afraid of God. I thought that He was always angry with me, wanting to punish me for what I did wrong. He was all about law and order—stern, strict, severe, and unfeeling. I had no concept of God as being Whom the Bible says He is: compassionate and gracious, slow to anger, and abounding in love. I had no idea that the prophet Isaiah talked about God in terms of a nurturing mother—caressing, holding, and caring for His children. I never read the countless references to God's tenderness, patience, and sensitivity to our weaknesses. I had no image of God as being someone who cared about me, who was concerned about me, and who wanted to be in relationship with me. I had never read or heard about His desire to be my *friend.* What was even more mind-boggling was my discovery that one of the chief purposes of my life was to be *His friend!*

What is friendship with God about? Jesus told us: "Greater love has no one than this, that he lay down his life for his friends. You are my friends if you do what I command. I no longer call you servants, because a servant does not know his master's business.

Instead, I have called you friends, for everything that I learned from my Father I have made known to you" (John 15:13–15).

In this passage, Jesus communicates three important truths for our lives. First, He gives us the ultimate test of friendship: the sacrifice of one life for another. I once read of a little girl at the Stanford Medical Hospital who was suffering from a rare and serious disease. The doctors said she had one and only one chance at surviving—a complete blood transfusion. And not just *any* blood transfusion, but one from her five-year-old brother. Her little brother had somehow survived the same disease and had developed the necessary antibodies to fight off the illness. His blood was her only chance of survival. The family knew that the little boy couldn't possibly understand all that was going on, so the doctor simply asked him if he would be willing to help his big sister by giving her his blood. The little boy looked at the doctor, then looked at his sister, and said, "All right, I will. I'll do it if it will help my sister."

So they set up the transfusion, and the little boy lay down in a bed next to his sister. He smiled at her as he saw his blood pass from his arm into hers. Then he looked up at the doctor, and with a trembling voice, he asked, "Will I start to die right away, or will it take a while?" Only then did they realize that he thought he had to give *all* of his blood and that it was his very *life* that he was giving to his sister.[10]

That's as deep as love gets. And Jesus as God in human form had that depth of love for you. He laid down his life for you and for me on the Cross. We should have hung there. The Cross was our death penalty, the punishment for our sins. But Jesus went in our place and paid our debt. He was your friend in the deepest and truest sense of the word.

The second thing that Jesus makes clear is that not only is He a friend, but that, through the Cross, we can be in a friendship with Him. In Christ, God makes it clear that He isn't some impersonal, unfeeling energy force that is unable to engage in relationship. He wants to be in an intimate, day-in, day-out relationship with us.

Third, Jesus tells us that we need to respond to His invitation to enter into that kind of friendship with Him. When two people are married, they exchange vows. Marriage is a mutual commitment. A bride and groom don't just talk about marriage; they commit to a marriage. It's no different with God. Through Christ, God offers us friendship—a friendship that is real, sacrificial, giving, intimate, and close. But Jesus said that we have to respond. He wants to be our friend, but we have to be willing to respond to His offer and vow to be *His* friend.

This is why the Book of James notes that "'Abraham believed God,' . . . and he was called God's friend" (James 2:23). When we use the word *believe* in English, we mean mental agreement or rational acceptance. But in the Bible, the word *believe* refers to more than mere intellectual assent; it speaks of a knowledge that leads to action. When the Bible says that Abraham believed, and as a result was God's friend, it means that Abraham not only believed in God intellectually, but he loved God, served God, spent time with God, and let God lead and shape his life. This is why James adds this footnote to the conversation: "Are there still some among you who hold that 'only believing' is enough? Believing in one God? Well, remember that the demons believe this too—so strongly that they tremble in terror!" (James 2:19 TLB). I can merely believe in the institution of marriage all day, yet never be married. Mere belief is meaningless; commitment is everything. And commitment involves a response.

During the Vietnam War, a young graduate of West Point was sent to lead a group of new recruits into battle. He did his job well, doing his best to keep his men from ambush and death. One night he and his men were overtaken by a battalion of Vietcong. He was able to get all of his men to safety—all but one. The one soldier left behind was severely wounded, and from their place of safety they could hear his cries for help. They all knew that returning for him would mean certain death. Suddenly the young lieutenant from West Point crawled toward the dying man. He made it to him and was able to drag him back. Just as he pushed the wounded man into the security of the trench, the young lieutenant caught a bullet in his back and was killed instantly.

Several months later, the rescued man returned to the United States. The parents of the dead hero invited the man whose life was spared at such a great cost to their family into their home for dinner. On the night of the dinner party, he arrived at their house drunk. He was loud and boisterous. He told dirty jokes and showed no concern for the grief of his hosts. The parents of the dead lieutenant did all they could to make it a worthwhile evening, but he ignored them all. At the end of that torturous visit, the obscene guest left. As her husband closed the door, the mother collapsed into tears and cried, "To think that our precious son had to die for some-body like that!" That soldier owed those parents the best that was in him. It was heartless indifference at its highest for him to give so little thought to what they had lost because of him. Considering the price that had been paid for his life, his ingratitude and behavior was beyond comprehension. He knew intellectually that his life had been saved by their son, but his life didn't reflect that he knew it, which means that he didn't really know it at all.[11]

Maybe now one of the most alarming statements that Jesus ever made will be understood in its full meaning: "Not all who sound religious are really godly people. They may refer to me as 'Lord,' but still won't get to heaven. For the decisive question is whether they obey my Father in heaven. At the Judgment many will tell me, 'Lord, Lord, we told others about you and used your name. . . .' But I will reply, 'You have never been mine'" (Matt. 7:21-23 TLB).

You may already be in a relationship with God as friend. You've tasted the rich intimacy of that relationship, the acceptance of God's grace, and the forgiveness of your sins. It's equally possible that you haven't, and perhaps now, for the first time, you realize what you are missing. You believe in God, but you're not His friend. You want to live a purposeful life, but you haven't gotten to first base on the foundational purpose of God for your life. So how do you go about that? It's called becoming a Christian. Contrary to what you might think, a Christian isn't someone who just leads a good life, goes to church, or was baptized as an infant. A Christian is someone who is a friend of God, and becoming that friend involves four steps.

FOUR IMPORTANT STEPS

First, own up to the fact that you aren't a friend of God. No rationalizations, no excuses, and no qualifications. Admit that you have rejected His leadership and are, quite frankly, a sinner in need of a Savior. The Bible says, "If we say that we have no sin, we are only fooling ourselves, and refusing to accept the truth" (1 John 1:8 TLB). The first step is to stop fooling yourself and to accept the truth that you have not been living as a friend of God.

The second step is to be willing to change. Not only must you be willing to admit your sins, you have to be willing to *turn* from them. You have to be willing to change the course of your life away from past patterns of behavior and toward what God wants you to be.

The third step of becoming God's friend is accepting the truth of God's Word. The Bible shows us that Jesus, Who was God in human form, took upon Himself our sin's death penalty and died in our place. Only through the Cross, where Christ's holiness was substituted for our sinfulness, can we experience forgiveness and friendship with God. The whole Bible is built around Christ's promise of forgiveness and friendship to sinners like you and me. The Bible says, "If you confess with your mouth that Jesus is Lord and believe in your heart that God raised him from the dead, you will be saved" (Rom. 10:9 NLT). You don't just believe intellectually; notice the language: "believe in your *heart.*" Being a friend of God takes your full commitment.

This leads to the fourth and final step. After you have admitted your sin, turned from it, and accepted the message of the Bible, you must then reach out and receive the gift of what Christ did for you through His death on the cross. The Bible says, "For the wages of sin is death, but the gift of God is eternal life in Christ Jesus our Lord" (Rom. 6:23). That gift was the forgiveness of our sins through the full payment of our sin penalty, which enables us to be a friend of God. God offers forgiveness to you as a gift, but it isn't yours until you reach out and take it.

So here's the question that faces you: Will you admit, change, believe, and receive the gift of salvation and a relationship with God through Christ? Saying yes is just *one prayer away,* because the Bible says, "Everyone who calls on the name of the Lord will be saved" (Rom. 10:13).

If you would like to become a Christian, a true friend of God, here's how to pray: Begin by telling God that you are a sinner. Admit that you fall short of His standards, His holiness, and His character. Just take a moment and say it to Him, in your own words, right where you are. Next, tell Him you want to be forgiven for those sins and receive an erased past and a new beginning. Now tell Him that you not only want Him as forgiver, but as leader. Invite His day-in, day-out management into your life. Finally, thank Him for forgiving you and for providing the leadership He will give to your life.

God has promised that when you ask Him to come into your life, He does. Something miraculous and of eternal significance has taken place in your heart. You have just taken the most important step toward fulfilling your ultimate purpose in life: a relationship with God as friend that enables you to become a saint, a soldier, and an ambassador. Now you're ready to take the next step toward discovering the specific purpose He has for your life, a purpose that begins with your life values.

CHAPTER FOUR

Determining Your Values

On Tuesday, October 3, 1995, practically everyone in America stopped what they were doing and gathered around a TV or a radio. The conclusion to one of the most riveting courtroom dramas in modern American history came to a stunning climax: A jury acquitted former football great O. J. Simpson of two counts of murder. The verdicts set him free 474 days after he was arrested and charged. Between 1:00 and 1:10 P.M., when the verdict was announced, everything came to a stop. People didn't work. They didn't go to class. They didn't make phone calls.

They listened to the verdict.

Newspaper accounts noted that airplanes had to wait because passengers wouldn't board before they heard. News conferences were postponed. The New York Stock Exchange and the Chicago Board of Trade slowed to a halt. The president of the United States, Bill Clinton, left the Oval Office to catch it with his secretary and aides. During that time period there was a ninety-three-million-watt increase as people turned on something, somewhere, to catch the news. Even the aircraft carrier *Independence,* sailing in the Persian Gulf, contacted the Navy Public Affairs office in Washington and piped the verdict through the carrier's sound system.

All to find out the decision of twelve jurors on the fate of one man.

Trials are interesting things. Evidence is put forth, arguments are considered, and testimony is heard. Then a decision, based on certain understandings of what is right or wrong, true or false, admissible or inadmissible, must be made. And make no mistake about the value-based nature of the decisions. Consider the Simpson verdict: People across America were divided on whether O. J. was guilty. They heard the same evidence and listened to the same testimony, but they came to very different conclusions. Even a second trial, for civil injuries, found O. J. guilty.

What Are Values?

Values are those things that make up, *for you,* what is right and what is wrong, what matters and what doesn't matter. Everybody has values; the problem is that not everybody agrees on what those values should *be,* much less where they should come from.

My friend Lee Strobel tells a story about a panel that convened in a conference room in order to find out what the simple value of integrity was all about. First, they invited a philosopher to come into the room. "Tell us," they said. "What is integrity?" The philosopher thought for a minute and then said, "Integrity is what you're like when nobody's around." The panel thanked him and agreed, "That's a pretty good answer."

Then they invited a businessman inside and asked for his definition. "In my world," he said, "integrity means a person is as good as his word." They thought that was a pretty good answer too!

Then they invited an attorney to enter. "What is integrity?" they asked him. The attorney's eyes cautiously scanned the room. He crept over to the door, opened it, looked outside to make sure nobody was listening, and then bolted it shut. He closed the windows, pulled down the shades, and then turned back to the panel. "Tell me," he whispered. "What do you *want* it to mean?"

A real value, of course, is not made up on the spot. An authentic, true value is something that is beyond us. It depends on a truth and a reality that is bigger than we are. That's why there has been so much talk at the beginning of the twenty-first century about *returning* to values that exist independently of what an individual may or may not embrace. Shootings at schools, racially motivated slayings, sexual assaults—we intuitively sense that only in authentic, lasting, core values is there hope. That's why Jesus spent so much time spelling out God's core values for individual life application, once even saying: "These words I speak to you are not incidental additions to your life. . . . They are foundational words, words to build a life on" (Matt. 7:24 MSG).

WHAT DO VALUES HAVE TO DO WITH MY LIFE PURPOSE?

How do your values tie in to your purpose for living? The answer is that your values are the moral compass by which you navigate through life. Your life values point you toward true north, setting your course. If values are timeless, eternal truths by which you guide your life, then the only way to fulfill your life purpose is to discover those foundational values. If you don't know your foundational values, then you won't have a basis by which to make decisions that will determine the very direction and destiny of your life.

This is the meaning behind the Bible's warning that "a double-minded man [is] unstable in all he does" (James 1:8). A double-minded person is unsure of what he stands for, blown this way and that by whatever comes along, and without a moral anchor. This person never follows a purpose in life, because he never establishes values to guide him along the waters of life. We need that outside reality, that transcendent sense of what is right and wrong, fact and fiction, significant and trivial.

Before Tom Lehman had the chance to prove himself on the PGA Tour, he had to enter the 1990 qualifying school (Q-school, as the pros call it) for the PGA Tour. During that high-pressure, all-or-nothing event, Lehman called a penalty stroke on himself. A stiff breeze caused Lehman's ball to move slightly after he addressed it, and the rules are clear: if the ball moves, you are penalized one stroke. The result? Lehman missed qualifying for the cut for the tour by—you guessed it—a *single stroke*. If the most important thing in Lehman's life was qualifying for the tour, if his values were based on success rather than faithfulness, he might not have called the penalty stroke. But his faith in Christ, coupled with the importance of living a purposeful life on the basis of *real* values, called him to honesty. His honesty resulted in waiting another year to qualify. "If a breach of the rules had occurred and I didn't call it on myself, I couldn't look at myself in the mirror," explained Lehman. "You're only as good as your word. And your word wouldn't be worth much if you can't even be honest with yourself." Lehman's loss at the Q-school sent him in 1991 to what's now known as the Nike Tour, where he set a tour record with seven tournament wins in a single season. The confidence he gained while waiting for his dream led to his subsequent PGA Tour victories. But that isn't what made his decision *best*. It was the fact that it reflected his values and resulted in faithfulness.[1]

Robertson McQuilken would understand. As a young man, he dreamed of becoming president of Columbia Bible College in Columbia, South Carolina. He adored his father, who had held this position, and wanted one day to take his place. McQuilken's dream came true, and he served as president of the college with distinction for many years. Then, just as he was about to enter the most productive years of his leadership, his wife began to show the first signs of Alzheimer's disease. In a matter of months, she not only lost the memory of much of their life together, but she was unable even to recognize Robertson as her husband.

Then McQuilken made a values-based, purposeful decision. He resigned the presidency of Columbia so he could give full-time care to his wife. Without hesitation he walked away from his lifelong dream as an act of love for his wife. Many told him there was no point in resigning. "Anyone can take care of your wife," they told him, "but not anybody can be president of Columbia." After all, they would often add, she didn't even recognize him when he came into the room.

McQuilken tried to explain his decision to his supporters and critics. He admitted that his wife didn't know who he was. But that wasn't the point, he told them. The really important thing was that *he* still knew who *she* was, and that he saw in her the same lovely woman he had married those many years ago. Then, with finality and conviction, he laid out the simple truth of a value upon which he had based his life: "And I promised to be there for her 'until death do us part.'"[2]

WHERE DO VALUES COME FROM?

Values are choices shaped by many competing forces, the strongest of which is undoubtedly the media. According to a study reported in the *New York Times,* the average person in America spends about eleven hundred hours a year watching broadcast TV, an additional five hundred hours watching cable, and three hundred hours listening to music.[3] The media's influence on human life cannot be underestimated. While television may not always tell you what to think, it certainly tells you what to think *about.* Today we are exposed to an estimated fifteen hundred commercial messages per day, with more than ten thousand magazines, six thousand radio stations, and four hundred television stations from which to choose.[4] Howard K. Smith, for years a commentator for ABC-TV, estimated that at least 80 percent of what the average citizen continues to learn about the world after leaving school "comes filtered through observations of the journalist."[5] And those observations are *not* value free.[6]

I observed the media's impact on values on Saturday, September 6, 1997, while I was doing my morning run. The gym where I work out has a bank of televisions, and each treadmill has a place for headphones so you can hook up and watch while you run. On this particular morning, I watched the entire *CNN Headline News* program from 8:30 to 9:00 A.M.

The first fifteen minutes were spent on Princess Diana. First, there was a story on her funeral. Then came a story on how her boys would handle her death and the media scrutiny of their lives. Then there was a report on the song that Elton John had composed for her funeral. Then there was footage of the bells pealing throughout England for her death. Then came another story on the eulogies that had been given at her burial. Then came two quick stories on other events: Hurricane Erica and the Space Station *Mir.* Then it went back to Elton John singing his new version of "Candle in the Wind." CNN then went right into its business news, sports segment, and entertainment coverage.

Now under normal circumstances, you would think that it was just a slow news day or that the death of Princess Diana was such a monumental event that it deserved to dominate the nation's leading cable newscast. But I happened to know something *else* had happened the night before, something that was never mentioned—*not even once.* Another woman died, a small, old Albanian woman named Agnes, better known to the world as Mother Teresa. The death of this Nobel Prize winner, and arguably the most beloved woman in the entire world, was completely ignored.

CNN wasn't alone. According to the Media Research Center, the coverage of Diana to Mother Teresa on the CBS evening news ran three to one; and on NBC, seven to one. *Newsweek* magazine had forty-seven pages on Diana, but only four on Mother Teresa. *Time* and *U.S. News & World Report* weren't much better.[7] But that wasn't all. Andrew Morton, on an ABC news story, said that Diana's death, and I quote, was "one of the most awful tragedies of the late 20th century, if not the greatest. . . . In her death something inside us had died. . . . People are grieving for lost hopes, lost dreams, lost ambitions."[8] When coupled with constant scenes of grief and crying, we were led to feel that this was a loss of cosmic proportions. Now, nothing against the tragic death of Diana, but not only was her death nowhere *near* the greatest tragedy that has occurred during the last fifty years—eclipsing such things as Vietnam, Chernobyl, Tiananmen Square, or the explosion of the Space Shuttle *Challenger*—but even when compared to the loss of other figures, such as Mother Teresa, Princess Di lived a life of very little significance. As has been quipped, she was just famous for being famous. But according to the media, Princess Di's life greatly overshadowed Mother Teresa's, and as a result, we were led to value her life that way. The talk was not that Mother Teresa would be made a saint, but that Princess Di would.[9]

There are other ways that the media can influence our values. One of the most powerful is through repetition, by putting certain choices or life styles before us over and over again until we become desensitized and accept those choices and life styles as normal. And if these choices are made by our favorite characters in a novel, actors in a film, performers on a music video, or actors on a television show, then we automatically associate positive feelings toward that behavior or choice.

Take sex, for example. *U.S News & World Report* did a study on a week's worth of prime-time viewing from ABC, CBS, NBC, and Fox. They found that of fifty-eight shows, almost half contained sexual acts or references to sex.[10] The Media Research Center has found that portrayals of premarital sex outnumbered sex within marriage by eight to one, and that "casual sex" was almost always approved of.[11] To say that this media portrayal hasn't impacted how we feel about sex, and from that, what is right and wrong about sex, would be naive. As George Lucas, one of the most successful filmmakers in Hollywood history, once said, "for better or worse . . . films and television tell us the way we conduct our lives, what is right and wrong."[12]

TODAY'S DOMINANT VALUES

So what are the dominant values of our day? I grow increasingly convinced that the late Francis Schaeffer was correct in stating that there are two widely accepted values: personal pleasure and personal prosperity.[13] The value of personal pleasure can be seen on virtually any talk show. Whatever life style is displayed, the conclusion is the same: If it makes them happy and doesn't seem to hurt anyone else, then it's okay. The value of personal pleasure says that what *I* want, what makes *me* happy, and what seems to give *me* the most satisfaction at *this* point in time is what is *right* and *true* and *good* and *noble.*

The second dominant value of our culture, personal prosperity, was baldly captured in the movie *Wall Street.* The character played by Michael Douglas gives a speech as a corporate leader in which he proclaims that greed is good. In a later movie, *Indecent Proposal,* Demi Moore and Woody Harrelson play a couple who are offered a million dollars if she would sleep with another man for one night. They accept. The movie never comments on whether the act itself is right or wrong, only whether it is okay for *their* relationship. The plot was whether the night of adultery would be *consequence* free; it was already assumed to be *value* free. Although most are quick to concede that money does not always purchase happiness, many remain convinced that getting more of it would be a good thing. When people were asked what single factor would most improve the quality of their lives, the most frequent answer in one American survey was "more money."[14]

VALUES FOR A PURPOSEFUL LIFE

The Bible gives an entirely different spin on the values of the world. The Bible, for example, says that pleasure is good. God smiles on it because He made it. But pleasure is not what God intended to be our reason to live, because operating your life on the value of pleasure alone is not investing in something that lasts. It's a superficial life. In fact, it's not really life at all. That's why the Bible says that "[by focusing on the] pleasures of living, the life is choked out of them, and in the end they produce nothing" (Luke 8:14 PHILLIPS). The Bible is not against money, but it goes against culture by contending that money isn't what life is about either. In fact, Jesus was clear when He said, "Real life and real living are not related to how rich we are" (Luke 12:15 TLB).

What Christ offers is a set of values that come from God Himself and that bring *life* itself. Transcendent values, ones that are bigger than we are, can speak to any and every situation, guiding us step by step toward significance and meaning. Notice how the apostle Paul speaks of this: "As long as you did what you felt like doing, ignoring God, you didn't have to bother with right thinking or right living, or right *anything* for that matter. But do you call that a free life? What did you get out of it? Nothing you're proud of now. Where did it get you? A dead end" (Rom. 6:20–21 MSG).

There is a fundamental life choice to be made when it comes to values: Christ or the world. As the Book of Job reminds us: "We should choose to follow what is right. But first of all we must define among ourselves what is good" (Job 34:4 TLB). The choice you make on this is important. The stakes are high. Following the values of the world will cause you to miss God's purpose for your life. You simply can't live by the world's values and still fulfill God's purpose for your life. Instead, you'll be like the infamous lemmings, small animals that live in northern Norway. Whenever lemmings go off in search of food, the majority of them die. There are so many that when they get near a cliff, some of them are pushed off the edge. And then, when some of them go over the edge, the rest feel they should follow. Soon an enormous herd of lemmings runs off the edge of the cliff to their deaths. It's a tragic scene: Instead of turning away from the crowd toward life, they follow the crowd and die.

WHAT ARE YOUR VALUES?

So what are your values? And how will they guide your life? First, settle the big question. Choose between Christ and the world.

Early in his ministry, Billy Graham wrestled with whether he was going to embrace the Bible as the inspired, revealed Word of God and source of truth for his life, or dismiss it as a fallible, unreliable book of merely human insight. He knew that everything in his life was on the line. The resolution came at a student conference at Forest Home, a retreat center in the San Bernadino Mountains near Los Angeles. Billy went for a walk in the serene pine forest. About fifty yards off a main trail, he sat for a long time on a large rock, his Bible spread open on a tree stump. Then he made his choice. "Oh God," he prayed, "I cannot prove certain things. I cannot answer some of the questions . . . some . . . people are raising, but I accept this Book by faith as the Word of God." I've been to Forest Home, and on a similar walk, I accidentally stumbled on the very rock upon which Graham made his lifelong values choice. A bronze tablet on the stone now commemorates his decision. Why such recognition? As Graham himself has observed, that single resolution "gave power and authority to my preaching that has never left me. The gospel in my hands became a hammer and a flame. . . . I felt as though I had a rapier in my hands and through it the power of the

Bible was slashing deeply into men's consciousness, leading them to surrender to God."[15] Settling the values question changed his life, and it changed the world.

Second, get specific about what your values mean for your life. Not many people have done this, so to get started, ask yourself the following questions:

- If I knew that tomorrow would be the last full day of my life, how would I spend the day?

- At the end of my life, what do I want to look back and say I've accomplished?

- If a list of adjectives were compiled to describe my life, what words would I like on that list?

- If I were to die tomorrow, what would I want people to remember as my most important achievement?

- Am I investing myself in those things that matter most to me?

- Is there any person or cause I would be willing to die for?

- If I were contemplating suicide, what are five reasons for not killing myself?

- What is vitally important to me, what has some importance, and what is a complete waste to me?

- If I were to write a letter to my children about what was most important in my life, what would I tell them?

- If only a single word could be written on my tombstone, what would that word be?

If you take the time to walk through these questions carefully and prayerfully, you will get very specific about what really matters to your life.

The third step is to evaluate your life. Take a long, hard look at your answers to these questions, and ask yourself: Is that how I'm living my life? If those are my values, is that what my calendar looks like? Is that reflected in my checkbook? Would the people around me say that's how I'm living? Is that how I spent my last week, my last month, or even my last few years? Have I *ever* lived this way?

The goal is to evaluate your life in order to bring it into harmony with your values. If I were to take a survey of typical Americans about what is important to their lives, I could guess what some of the top answers would be: God, marriage, family, and health. But if you could go to those people and poke around a little, I think we all know what we would find. The ones who say their relationship with God is the most important thing aren't developing that relationship with very much intensity. The ones who say that nothing's more important than their family are the same ones who contribute to the statistic that the average American father spends less than five minutes of true, face-to-face time with his children a day. People who say that they value their marriage are the same ones who contribute to a 25 percent divorce rate. The ones who say their health is so vital to their lives are the same ones who have made America the obesity capital of the world. You see, there is a huge gap between what we *say* matters to us and how we really live. Our values have become divorced from our life purpose.

Whenever there is a separation between values and practice, things break down. The way we want things to be *aren't,* and the way we hope things will go *don't.* In ancient China, the people desired security from the barbaric, invading hordes to the north. To get this protection, they built what is now known as the Great Wall of China. And this wall was, and still is, truly great! It's thirty feet high, eighteen feet thick, and more than fifteen hundred miles long! The goal of the Chinese was to build an absolutely impenetrable defense—too high to climb over, too thick to break down, and too long to go around. But during the first one hundred years of the wall's existence, China was successfully invaded not once, not twice, but *three times.* And it wasn't the wall's fault. During all three invasions, the barbaric hordes never climbed over the wall, broke it down, or went around it; they simply bribed a gatekeeper and then marched right in through an open door. The purpose of the wall failed because of a breakdown in values.[16]

A person who lives a purposeful life determines his or her values and then lives by them. Every year, Americans take a day to celebrate the life and work of Dr. Martin Luther King, Jr. His role in history is secure, but when I think of the civil rights movement, he's not the first hero that comes to my mind. I think of a forty-two-year-old woman who was on her way home from work on a cold December day in 1955. Getting on a public bus, she paid her fare and sat down in her. She was just glad to rest, because her legs were tired. But as the bus filled with passengers, the driver told her that she would have to stand and give her seat to another passenger. Why? Because she was *black,* and more seats were needed for *whites.*

She wasn't an activist or a radical—just a quiet, conservative, churchgoing woman with a nice family and a decent job as a seamstress. But she didn't move. Maybe it was the injustice of it all. Maybe it was the years of persecution and abuse that she and millions of others had suffered for no other reason than the color of their skin. Maybe she was tired of being treated as a second-class citizen, having to drink from certain fountains, go to certain bathrooms, and being forced into certain schools. Whatever ran through her heart and mind, one thing was clear: *This was wrong.*

So she remained in her seat.

The bus driver began yelling at her, telling her to move. And then the other passengers began to yell at her, push at her, and even curse her. But she stayed right where she was. The driver stopped the bus, got off, and called the police. When they arrived, they hauled her off to jail. But what they really did was haul her off into history. Because that woman was Rosa Parks, and her stand for what was right—or her *sit* for what was right—ignited the entire civil rights movement.

She didn't get on that bus looking for trouble or planning to make some kind of political statement. She just wanted to go home, like everybody else. And as a Christian, she knew she was made in the image of God. She knew she had dignity and worth. She knew she was a precious daughter of God who was called to live a life for Him. But she needed her values to come to the fore when it came time to enter into what she now sees as one of the grand purposes of her life. And the world has never been the same.

The good news is that living a purposeful, value-driven life is a journey open to all of us. In the film *Regarding Henry,* Harrison Ford played a lawyer who was injured in a robbery. He was cutthroat, dishonest, unfaithful to his wife, and distant from his daughter. But the accident caused him to lose his memory, and so he started his entire life over again, this time as a different man. The accumulation of life choices that had led him toward one set of values were replaced by a fresh set of choices. Before the accident, he had ruthlessly suppressed evidence that would have awarded a poor family a medical malpractice settlement. After discovering the importance of honesty and values, he quit his job and went back to that poor family to give them the evidence they needed to win the case against his former firm. When he went to the door and handed over the documents, the shocked wife said, "I don't get it. What changed?"

Ford simply said, "I did."

CHAPTER FIVE

Discovering Your Strengths

Have you ever looked at a couple and said, "They were just *made* for each other"? Perhaps you have spoken to someone about a job opportunity and said, "This job is *you.*" Or maybe you've seen how someone has reacted and said, "That's just how he is wired." It's as if deep down we know that there is a relationship between who we are and what we are to do, between *how* God made us and the life plan God has for us. Guess what—you're right. That is *exactly* the way it works. You were made, crafted, and designed by a Creator who put *into* your creation much of the blueprint for your life.

Think of it like your DNA.

DNA, which stands for deoxyribonucleic acid, is the basic material in the chromosomes of the cell nucleus. It contains your genetic code and transmits your hereditary pattern. From a physical standpoint, DNA is the makeup of who you are. It determines everything from your hair color to your height.

There's another kind of DNA that flows through our veins, but this kind is deeper than merely physical—it's psychological, emotional, and spiritual. This kind of DNA, which is every bit as distinctive and representative for your life as your physical DNA, stands for something a little easier to remember, and *say*, than deoxyribonucleic acid. This DNA stands for your "D"—desires, your "N"—nature, and your "A"—abilities.[1] Let's talk about all three, because the purpose of your life is simply to be who you are, beginning with your natural gifts and abilities.

GIFTS AND ABILITIES

Several years ago, a movie called *Chariots of Fire* captured the attention of millions of people. If you saw the movie, you remember that it tells the true story of Eric Liddell, an Olympic runner from Scotland in the thirties. In the film, Liddell's sister, Jenny, questions him about why he was going to run in the Olympics instead of pursue a career as a missionary in China. He takes her for a walk in the highlands, pauses to turn and view the city of Edinburgh, and then says, "Jenny, you've got to understand. I believe that God made me for a purpose, for China. He also made me *fast*, and when I run, I feel His pleasure." So he goes to China, but he also *runs*, because his athletic ability was a gift from God.

God made each of us fast somewhere, and when we run in that area, we too can feel His pleasure. As the Bible teaches, "God has given each of us the ability to do certain things well" (Rom. 12:6 TLB). But we can neglect to follow our natural bent, even when it was once clear to us that we had natural ability in that particular area. Even more tragic is when we allow the expectations or demands of others to force us in directions that God never intended.

So take a moment and reflect on what you do well. What have others affirmed about you? It has often been suggested to think in terms of ten-year increments. For example, write down two or three things you were naturally good at during your elementary school years, then your high school years, then your twenties, and, if needed, your thirties and beyond. The reason you ought to do it that way is that there may have been some natural talents and abilities God gave you that have been buried or overlooked for *years*—and for all of the wrong reasons.

Another reason this "time inventory" is so crucial is that many of our gifts and abilities—some would say *all* of our gifts and abilities—began to present themselves at a very early age. If you could turn the clock back on a successful salesperson, you'd probably find someone who ran the neighborhood lemonade stand. If you could walk through the early scrapbook of a famous actor or actress, you'd likely find videos of him or her in the school play or putting on a backyard show.[2]

There was a boy who filled his playroom from one end to the other with thousands and thousands of toy soldiers arrayed for battle. He organized wars and maneuvered battalions into action. Using peas and pebbles, his toy soldiers stormed forts and destroyed bridges. He even designed real water tanks to engulf the advancing foe. The boy played with an interest and passion for strategy that made it clear that this was no ordinary child's game. Later, with his brother Jack, he built a log house and dug a ditch around it that they filled with water. Then a working drawbridge was added, and the fort was stormed. The boy's name? Winston Churchill, whose wartime leadership kept England from falling to Nazi Germany during World War II.[3]

But that's not all there is to gifts and abilities. Beyond natural gifts and abilities, there are *spiritual* gifts and abilities. The Bible teaches that everyone who becomes a Christian receives the indwelling presence of the Holy Spirit, who gives you at least one spiritual gift to be used for the equipping of His church. Notice how this is talked about in the Book of Ephesians: "Christ has given each of us special abilities—whatever he wants us to have out of his rich storehouse of gifts" (Eph. 4:7 TLB). And each of us has our own unique gift mix. There isn't one gift, or one ability, that all are to have or that is better than another. We each have what God intended us to have. As taught in 1 Corinthians 7:7, "Each man has his own gift from God; one has this gift, another has that."

So what exactly *are* these gifts?

Here's the simplest definition I know: A spiritual gift is a supernatural *ability* to develop a particular *capability* for making a difference with your life through serving.[4] They can be along the lines of natural gifts and abilities, such as teaching, administration, or leadership. But they can also involve such things as discernment, wisdom, mercy, and giving. What makes them *spiritual* gifts, not just natural talents, is that God will supernaturally empower these gifts for maximum impact as you develop and pursue them in your life. But what if you don't know what your spiritual gifts might be? The good news is that increasing numbers of churches are offering programs and classes, accompanied with helpful self-testing materials, that will assist you in discovering your God-given spiritual gifts.[5]

Now here's what's important about your gifts and abilities in regard to experiencing a purposeful life. It's not just that you have them, but that they tell you *what* to *do!*

If you're a leader, you're supposed to lead!

If you're an administrator, you're supposed to administrate!

If you're gifted as a counselor, counsel!

If you're a teacher, teach!

If you're an artist, have a way with business, have abilities in science or medicine, know how to serve others and put them at ease, can manage buildings or properties, or could sell ice to inhabitants of the North Pole, don't ignore it! Those are signs as to what you are to do.

PASSIONS AND DESIRES

But gifts and abilities are only part of your DNA. Next up are your passions and desires. Your passions are those topics or activities that you care about on a deep, even emotional level. When you think about them, your eyes light up. When you do anything related to it, you get energized.

Now some passions are superficial, or at best, temporary, like the passion of the folks who camped out for days during May 1999 to get tickets to the new *Star Wars* movie. But the kind of passion that defines your life, directs your life, and points you toward what God wants your life to be about is on another level. It's the kind of passion that reveals your deepest emotional heartbeat. Want to get in touch with yours? Just ask yourself some of these questions:

- What do I really care about?

- When I have an afternoon all to myself, free of family and work responsibilities, how do I want to spend it?

- When I look around and think something needs to be changed, what area does my mind tend to travel toward?

- What do I dream about?

- What would I do to make every morning feel like Christmas Day?

- If I could leave my mark on any area of life, what would it be?

Some of these questions are similar to the value questions raised in the previous chapter, but there is a key distinction: these questions point you to a specific area or interest that reflects your heart. There's an interesting line in the Bible that says to "watch over your heart; *that's* where life starts" (Prov. 4:23 MSG). Perhaps we could risk a rephrase without doing an injustice to the text: "Follow your heart; that's where your life will be found!"

He was only five or six years old when he discovered he had a voice. It was a fine voice, but nothing sensational. *But he loved to sing!* So he would go into his room and close the door and, at the top of his lungs, sing in his child's voice "La donna é mobile." Of the sixteen families in his building, he recalls that at least fourteen of them would yell at him to shut up. But he followed his heart and found his life. His name? Luciano Pavarotti.[6]

Now here's how your passion plays into experiencing a purposeful life. While your gifts and abilities point you toward *what* to do, your passions and desires point you toward *where* to do it! You may have a teaching gift, but where do you put it into play? If your passion involves children, there is your direction—you should explore *teaching* with *children!*

See how this works?

Take your gift, which is *what* you are to do, and link it with your passion, which is *where* you are to do it. But what if you are unclear about your passion? One of the saddest statements I have ever heard, yet I know reflects the feeling of many, was made by a woman who heard me speak on this topic and then asked me, "But what if you don't have anything in your life that you are passionate about?" My advice is to go back over the first few chapters of this book and get passionate about what *God* is passionate about. Become filled with *His* passion. Catch the vision of what God is doing in this world. There is a revolution afoot, and God is on the loose. You are a child of God with a high calling on your life as a soldier and ambassador. Discover your gift and begin using it as God leads in areas of need. Then await the opening of the door of your heart as God introduces you to the place where your service meets an emotional heartbeat of your own within the heartbeat of His cause.

PERSONALITY AND NATURE

The third major mark of your "DNA" that plays into the purpose of your life has to do with your personality, or your inner nature. Under the inspiration of the Holy Spirit, the psalmist wrote: "You [God] created my inmost being; you knit me together in my mother's womb. . . . I am fearfully and wonderfully made" (Ps. 139:13–14). God created everything about you, even your *inmost being*. That phrase was the ancient way of talking about your inner world, the very nature of who you are and how you're wired.

We all have a nature, a personality, that is unique to who we are.[7] For example, we can be extroverts or introverts. Extroverts get their energy from social contact and want to be with people all the time. Introverts get their energy from being alone, and too much time with people can leave them emotionally drained. The introvert wants a vacation to get him away from the world, while the extrovert goes knocking at all the hotel rooms so he can introduce himself.

A second way our personalities can be unique is whether we lean more toward the intuitive or the sensing side of things. This deals with how you take in information and deal with problems. The intuitive person focuses on ideas and possibilities. They're the big-picture type, going on hunches and gut-level perceptions. Sensing people need the facts. They want all of the pertinent data. While the intuitive person goes on imagination, the sensing person goes on details. They are more oriented on figures, charts, and balance sheets than ideas and possibilities.

A third way we can be differentiated is whether we are thinkers or feelers. This is a difference that addresses how we make decisions. Thinkers make their decisions on the basis of clear logic and practicality. Feelers are more people oriented and go on emotion.

A final set of personality differences you often see has to do with basic life orientation, whether you are structured or unstructured, or what some would call judging or perceiving. Structured, or judging, people like a predictable routine. They thrive on organization, deadlines, rules, and policies. They like to make a plan and stick to it. Unstructured, or feeling, people like spontaneity. They *hate* routines, rules, deadlines, and plans. They want the day to unfold naturally and see what might happen. They're unpredictable and often disorganized. They like to play life as it comes.

So which are you?

I'm right on the borderline between being an introvert and an extrovert. Almost all of my skills and abilities are extrovert oriented, but my emotional energy is often restored when I withdraw from people. The other sets are much more defined: I'm more intuitive than sensing, more of a thinker than a feeler, and more structured than unstructured. If you're familiar with the famous Myers-Briggs testing categories, I'm basically an ENTJ (extrovert, intuitive, thinker, judger), with the "E" part being the most diluted.

The Bible says that my nature and personality was given to me by God! *And so was yours.* Following our internal bent matters: If your gifts and abilities direct you toward *what* to do, and your passions and desires point you toward *where* to do it, your personality helps you know *how* to do it! So if you're an extrovert, you're going to want to put your gifts and passions into play in a way that involves people. And that's okay! That's why the Bible says, "God works through different [people] in different ways" (1 Cor. 12:6 PHILLIPS).

PAST EXPERIENCES

There is a fourth area that should be considered, beyond your basic "DNA" makeup, that can often be strategic in terms of life strengths. This area has to do with your life experiences: your background, upbringing, and the unique circumstances that have shaped your life. The Bible says: "We know that all that happens to us is working for our good if we love God and are fitting into his plans" (Rom. 8:28 TLB). This does not mean that all things are good, only that God will use what has happened to us for good if we place it in His hands and trust Him with our lives. Think of the experiences of your past—your educational experiences, vocational experiences, family experiences, spiritual or ministry experiences, as deposits in an account. These deposits can, and often should, be withdrawn in order to evaluate and invest.

Even the traumatic ones.

I once heard of a couple whose baby died of sudden infant death syndrome. Their pastor conducted the funeral, and through that event, both parents came to Christ. Several months later, another young mother lost her baby. The pastor went to the family and tried to comfort them, but nothing he said or did seemed to be of much help. But at the funeral, the mother who had lost her child just a few months earlier stepped up to the other mother's side, put her arm around her, and said, "I went through this, and I know what you are going through. In the middle of the darkness, God called me, and I came to Him. He has comforted me, and He will comfort you!" That first mother did more for the second mother than anyone else could have possibly done, because she had traveled the road of suffering herself. And she has helped countless mothers ever since. As the apostle Paul wrote in 2 Corinthians, "[God] comes alongside us when we go through hard times, and before you know it, he brings us alongside someone else who is going through hard times so that we can be there for that person just as God was there for us" (2 Cor. 1:3–4 MSG).

WHAT ABOUT MY JOB?

One of the first questions to develop in the mind of people seeking out their life purpose is the relation of their life strengths to their jobs. We wonder if our purpose should *be* our job, and what should we do if our job doesn't go along with our gift mix? Interestingly, the word *vocation* is from the Latin *vocare,* which means "calling." Only in recent years have we separated the idea of our jobs from the call of God on our lives; in other words, from our purpose. Now we don't think of our work in terms of a calling. It seldom enters our minds that our work should reflect who we are and what God created us to do and to be. If anything, we have let our *jobs* define who we are. So we say that we *are* a teacher, a doctor, a lawyer, a salesperson, or a computer technician—because that's what we *do*. In truth, we might not *be* those things at all.

Let's examine the life of a man we will call Bob. He went to college for one simple reason: to be able to get a well-paying job. No search for truth, no desire to read the classics, it was pure economics and pragmatism. And when it came time to settle in on an area of study, like many of his classmates, Bob chose a major on the basis of what would allow him to find a job with a high salary and strong potential for promotion. After scanning the landscape of emerging careers, he settled on marketing and management. After graduation, Bob investigated which companies offered the best pay, best benefits, and best opportunities for career advancement. The job itself didn't matter as much as the money. After marrying his college sweetheart, Bob began his career.

At first it was fine. There was a novelty about wearing a suit and tie and carrying a briefcase to an office every morning. Proposals and contracts, meetings and deadlines, and trips and presentations filled him with a sense of self-importance. And then there was that special reward, that reminder of what it was all about: his paycheck. The house, the cars, the boat, the vacations, everything was falling into place, and life was good. But as time went on, something Bob never planned on began to take shape. He began to realize that five out of every seven days of his life were given to his job. Weekends were great, but Mondays rolled around with incredible regularity. Week in, and week out. Year in, and year out.

Decisions made out of economics and pragmatism were now determining his entire life investment. When he started, he thought that what mattered in life would be gained by his salary, so he had built his entire life around making sure that his salary would reach its optimum potential. But over time the toys and the weekends and the vacations seemed diminishing compensation for the growing sense of routine and lack of fulfillment Bob felt in his work. So as he entered his late thirties, Bob caught an early case of midlife crisis.

Bob's problem isn't unique. It's the way lots of folks feel, or will soon start to feel. Many of us went to college and chose our majors based on what paid the most and where the jobs were. And when we entered the marketplace, we chose our jobs based on what was offered to us and who paid the most. Then we spend our careers climbing up the ladder toward greater levels of financial and material success. And all during that process we never stop to ask ourselves the most important question of all: Is this what I am supposed to do with my life? Is this my purpose? Interestingly, the Bible says in Ecclesiastes: "There is nothing better for men than that they should be happy in their work, for that is what they are here for" (Eccles. 3:22 TLB). But that simply cannot happen apart from a sense of purpose. So instead of the idea that "You are what you do," the radical perspective of the Bible is that you are to *do* what you *are!* [8] And not just in relation to spiritual gifts and ministry within the church, but your *vocation itself.* So ask yourself the following four questions: First, does my job reflect my *values?* Second, does my job use my *gifts and abilities?* Third, does my job involve my passions and interests? Fourth, does my job fit my *personality?* If not, then you are probably not within the call of God on your life.

RADICAL RETHINKING

At sixty-two years of age, he startled his friends and challenged fellow executives when he did the "unthinkable." In a nation where a man's status is largely measured by position and power, Suh Sang-rok quit the number-two job at one of South Korea's largest conglomerates to wait tables in a restaurant. But the philosophy of this former executive was simple: Position is not important. *Any* job is honorable. "If you like your job, no matter how much or how little it pays, you can accommodate—that is honorable," says Suh. "Being in a high-level position that you dislike or are not qualified for is dishonorable." Early on, Suh said that his friends voiced concerns that he was causing them to lose face. "But now people . . . are calling me a genius!" And when his former coworkers asked him what they were supposed to do if he, the vice-chairman of their company, became a waiter, Suh quickly responded, "How about assistant waiter?"[9]

Tom Paterson writes of a neighbor who admitted to him that he ran his roofing company because he married the daughter of the owner. "That's the only reason," he confessed. "I hate my job."

So Paterson asked him, "What would you really like to be doing?"

"I'd like to be teaching high-school history," he said.

"Why don't you do that?" Paterson asked.

The man simply said, "I'd lose too much."

"Consider what you would gain," was Paterson's reply.[10]

We are only satisfied when we work where we were meant to

work, and that involves taking into consideration the kind of person God made you. This will include your values, abilities, interests, and personality. Of course, no job encompasses all of these to perfection, and there are times that we must simply take what we can get in order to survive. But the goal is to understand that our vocation *is* our calling, and that the two should never become separate. But what if they *have* become divorced in your life? I don't know if this will surprise some of you, but I think the answer, while being responsible to your financial obligations and the emotional needs of your family, is to find another job. And it won't be easy. It may mean switching to another division in your company. It may mean leaving your company altogether. It may mean starting over completely, even going back to school. These are hard roads to take, but if you are a round peg trying to fit into a square hole, you will never be happy. Unless you work in a way that reflects whom God made you to be, you can never operate out of a sense of purpose for your life. As Dorothy Sayers has written, "Work is not, primarily, a thing one does to live, but the thing one lives to do. It is, or it should be, the full expression of the worker's faculties, the thing in which he finds spiritual, mental, and bodily satisfaction, and the medium in which he offers himself to God." [11]

No matter what your vocation, to have a sense of purpose in life, you need to feel that you're doing what you are, that you're honoring God by being true to how He designed you, and that you are fulfilling some sense of what you were meant to do and to be. Whether your vocation is a homemaker or software developer, teacher or insurance salesperson, advertising executive or investment banker, you have to ask yourself: *Does this matter? Am I making a difference? Is there a purpose in doing this for my life work?* If it fits your values, personality, abilities, and interests, the answer can be yes in almost any job. This is much of the meaning behind the often-quoted verse that says: "Whatever you do, work at it with all your heart, as working for the Lord, not for men" (Col. 3:23).

Mr. Holland's Opus was an interesting movie. Mr. Holland wanted fame and fortune as a musical composer but instead resigned himself to the life of a music teacher in a high school. He dreamed of composing a symphony but ended up writing only report cards. At the end of his career, upon retirement, he learned an important truth: He *had* composed a symphony, a grand opus consisting of the beautiful notes sounded by the lives of the students he touched. He learned it was the most important score he could have written. Tragically, he didn't see this until the very end.

But the purpose is not found merely in the exercising of your gifts in their proper place, but in wedding that calling with your *ultimate* calling. God's goal is to take full-time saints, soldiers, ambassadors, and friends and disguise them as lawyers, doctors, and real estate brokers.

An inner-city church had an annual student recognition day. Normally, students would share about their educational experiences and then the pastor would get up and offer a few closing words. One year, the pastor's words were a bit alarming. He stood up in front of all the young graduates and proud parents and said, "Children, you're going to die! You may not *think* you're going to die, but you're going to die! One of these days they're going to take you out to the cemetery, drop you in a hole, throw some dirt on your face, and go back to the church and eat potato salad."

Not exactly your normal commencement address. But he was just warming up.

"When you were born, you alone were crying, and everybody else was happy. The important question I want to ask is this: When you die are you alone going to be happy, leaving everybody else crying? The answer depends on whether you live to get *titles* or *testimonies*. Will they list your degrees and awards, or will they tell about what you meant to their lives? Will you leave behind a newspaper column telling people how important you were, or will you leave behind crying people who give their testimonies about how they've lost the best friend they ever had? Will they talk about all the boards you sat on and things you owned, or will they talk about all the money you gave away that made a difference in this world?

"There's nothing wrong with titles. Titles are good things to have. But if it ever comes down to a choice between a title or a testimony, *go for the testimony.*"

And then he started to preach what some would call a poetic rip. He went through the Bible talking about those who had titles and the ones who had testimonies.

"Pharoah may have had the title . . .
but Moses had the testimony!
Nebuchadnezzzar may have had the title . . .
but Daniel had the testimony!
Queen Jezebel may have had the title . . .
but Elijah had the testimony!"

And he went on and on, getting a little louder each time, until he got to the climax, where he said,

"Pilate may have had the title . . ."

And then pausing for what seemed like an eternity, he thundered,

". . . but my Jesus had the testimony!"

And then he asked a single question: *What will it be for your life?*[12]

CHAPTER SIX

Defining Your Mission

Few events are more inspiring than the Olympic games. When they came to the United States in 1996, I joined with thousands who had lined the streets of Charlotte to watch the Olympic torch make its trip down to Atlanta. Olympic athletes tend to motivate people to want to accomplish more, to try harder in their lives. There's something about seeing ordinary people accomplish extraordinary things through hard work and determination that deeply inspires people all over the world. It causes an eleven-year-old boy to go out for his first five-kilometer run around a YMCA track, with images of cruising to gold medals in the 200- and 400-meter races racing through his mind. A thirteen-year-old girl is challenged to think of swimming in a backstroke competition or balancing on a beam. Even those of us who are a bit older can look at individuals such as Carl Lewis, who at age thirty-five soared through the air with a jump in the 1996 games that won him first place in the long jump and his ninth gold medal in four Olympics.

We walk away from the Olympics moved, wanting to reach for the gold ourselves, somewhere in our own lives. Following the Atlanta games, a woman who was interviewed said that it made her want to live her life with a bigger *mission.*[1]

Her choice of words was insightful. Having a sense of mission in your life is crucial to any level of achievement, particularly to the greatest achievement of all: *living purposefully.* Knowing who you are as a human, discovering your identity in Christ, even connecting with your individual strengths and values can remain impotent apart from being channeled toward an identifiable *aim.*

What's a Life Mission?

When the apostle Paul talked about this in his own life, he said, "I only want to complete my mission and finish the work that the Lord Jesus gave me to do" (Acts 20:24 TEV). To experience a purposeful life, you have to move from your basic purpose in life, which you share with every other human being, to your *specific* purpose in life—your mission—which is yours and yours alone.

You might think of your mission in military terms. It is one thing to know the *purpose* and *ability* of a particular military unit, such as an infantry division; it is another to know the specific *mission* you are trying to accomplish *as* that infantry division. In the same way, it is one thing to understand your foundational life identity (made by God in His image) and foundational life purpose (friend, saint, soldier, and ambassador), as well as the gifts you have been given, but it is another to know what you are trying to accomplish *through* those basic purposes, strengths, and identities. What is it you are devoted to doing with your life in *light* of your identity and purpose, gifts, and placement? What is your specific *objective*?

Another way of thinking about it is along the lines of a business. Let's say that a particular investment group agrees to finance five teams to open restaurants in select cities. Each team is asked to purchase food wholesale and then create a retail establishment where that food is prepared and sold for a profit. The purpose is the same for each: to open and operate a restaurant. Each team has been equipped to do so, but when it comes to *designing* those restaurants and developing the respective menus, enormous divergence begins. One chooses to open a McDonald's franchise. Another goes upscale with a Morton's of Chicago steakhouse. The third decides to pursue "eatertainment" with a Rainforest Cafe. The fourth goes with a sushi bar, and the last decides to offer calabash-style seafood.

Each was given a foundational purpose, along with the resources necessary to fulfill it, but each *pursued* the fulfillment of that purpose with great distinction. Like a restaurant owner, you can understand your basic purpose in life and be given specific gifts and abilities that point you toward unique investments, but you need to define the specific way your life is going to *express* those dynamics. And that's where your mission comes in. How has God called you to express the purpose of your life?

Now it's very important to note that a mission is more than a goal. If you ask some people what their mission in life is, they'll say things like, "To retire at forty," "To make lots of money," "To graduate," "To get married," or "To own my own business." But those are not life missions, they are simply goals. Goals can *support* your mission, but they are not the mission itself. A mission is based on God's purposes for your life. It expresses who you are and how God made you. It manifests how you, as an individual, take the foundational purposes of God and unite them with your unique creation in order to make the optimum contribution and impact. A mission takes your many roles and gifts, values and experiences, and ties them all together in a single aim. As the Bible reminds us, "Don't act thoughtlessly, but try to find out and do whatever the Lord wants you to" (Eph. 5:17 TLB).

And your mission must be all encompassing. You can't just say, "My job is my life mission." Why? Because your mission has to be bigger than that. You can lose your job, but you can never lose your mission. You can't say, "Raising my children is my mission," because the call of God on your life is much larger than a season of life. Your mission can, and should, include roles and responsibilities, but not be solely defined by them. The vision for the mission of your life must be larger. I once read of a full-time homemaker who was asked in a condescending manner what she *did*. She replied: "I am socializing two *Homo sapiens* into the dominant values of the Judeo-Christian tradition so they might be transformers of the social order into the kind of eschatological utopia God willed for us from before the foundation of the earth." Then she smiled sweetly and asked, "And what is it *you* do?"[2]

WHY IS A MISSION SO IMPORTANT?

You might think that knowing your foundational purposes in life is enough to lead a purposeful life. Just engage yourself in being an ambassador or soldier, and use your gifts wherever there is a need. I disagree. Nothing becomes *dynamic* until it becomes *specific*. I once heard a professor at Stanford University make this point at a seminar on leadership. He noted that there was a big difference between having the *idea* of getting into shape, even having the knowledge of getting into shape, as opposed to saying that you are going to enter and then win your age division in the Hawaiian Open Ironman Triathlon.[3] And he's right. Having a general understanding of your life purpose is one thing; taking that purpose and investing it in a unique mission is another.

But that's not all. Taking the extra step of seeking out a specific life mission will help you *persevere* in living purposefully. On July 4, 1952, a thirty-four-year-old woman waded into the water off of the coast of Catalina Island and began to swim toward the California shore. Her goal was to be the first woman to swim the famous twenty-one-mile strait. Her name was Florence Chadwick, and she had already become the first woman to swim the English Channel. The water that morning was numbing cold, and the coast of California was covered in fog. In fact, the fog was so thick that she could hardly see the boats that were escorting her attempt. More than fifteen hours later, numbed with the cold, she asked to be taken out of the water.

Her mother, who was also her trainer, encouraged her to go on, telling her that she was close to the shore. But all Florence could see was the fog. She said, "Take me out." After she got out of the water, she came to the disappointing realization that her mother was right. She had been only a half-mile from the coast. When interviewed by reporters, she said, "If I could have seen the shore, I might have made it." Your mission not only gets you in the water, but it helps you see the shore so that you can keep on swimming.[4]

DEVELOPING A SENSE OF MISSION

So how do you develop a sense of mission in your life? By coming to a clear, concise understanding of how you are going to invest your purposes. Consider the following five components, beginning with the foundational purposes of your life.

We have been called to certain basic purposes in life. The first and foremost foundational purpose is knowing and loving God. Jesus said, "Love the Lord your God with all your heart, soul, and mind. This is the first and greatest commandment" (Matt. 22:37-38 TLB). We were made to enjoy a personal, loving, intimate relationship with God. Our life mission begins with knowing Him—not just knowing *about* Him, but truly *knowing* Him in the context of a personal relationship.

The second basic purpose God has for your life is to become like Christ. In Romans, we read that "from the very beginning God decided that those who came to him . . . should become like

His Son" (Rom. 8:29 TLB). In fact, the word *Christian* literally means "little Christ."

The third basic purpose of life is to use what you have been given by God to help others. The Bible says: "God has given each of you some special abilities; be sure to use them to help each other, passing on to others God's many kinds of blessings" (1 Pet. 4:10 TLB). You and I are called to make a contribution with our lives, and that contribution is tied to our basic abilities, passions, personality, and experiences. That's why we have them, to be used!

The final foundational desire of God for every life is to tell others about Him. As the apostle Paul declared, "Life is worth nothing unless I use it for doing the work assigned me by the Lord Jesus—the work of telling others the Good News about God's mighty kindness and love" (Acts 20:24 TLB). This means that your basic life purpose involves a life *message*. God wants to say something to the world through you, and only you can say it in your way because there is no one else like you, and there never will be. Any mission in life will have these four purposes as its foundation.

From this, as a second component, let your mission take shape through the direction and application of your life values, as opposed to mere self-interest. Martin England was a white, Southern insurance salesman. He learned that Dr. Martin Luther King, Jr., the great civil rights leader, was not covered with an adequate life insurance policy. And it bothered him. In fact, he worried about it almost every day. He was fueled by a set of values that led him to see his role in insurance as a way to provide care for people in a time of great sadness and sorrow and need.

And he cared about Martin Luther King.

So he began to try to contact Dr. King to sell him the kind of family protection plan that would insure the future well-being of King's family, should anything happen to him. It wasn't easy getting to King, but he felt it was important. So he followed King for weeks, trying to tell the civil rights leader that he had a gigantic and urgent need. Finally, he got his opportunity. And when he did, he sat Martin Luther King down, explained his need for life insurance, and got the necessary papers signed. And then, not long afterward, an assassin's bullet pierced King's body. But because someone lived a mission based on values, King's death was not compounded by leaving behind a destitute family.[5]

Third, a specific life mission should reflect your natural strengths and abilities, and most importantly, your spiritual gifts. God gave you those distinguishing characteristics for a reason, and God's mission for your life will incorporate those qualities. If your gifts involve hospitality, then any mission statement for your life would involve taking that gift of hospitality, in light of your personality type, and ensuring it is optimally leveraged for the sake of the kingdom of God.

Next, your mission should reflect your passions. There was once an eccentric inventor who witnessed the deaths of a number of children who drank contaminated milk. That ignited a passion within him that he used to develop a mission to find a way to preserve milk so that children's lives could be saved. His name was Gail Borden, and that mission led him to found the now well-known Borden's Milk and Ice Cream company. But without his passion, he would

96

not have discovered his mission. In the nineteenth century, when countless surgery patients died from infections caused by unsanitary conditions, a young man named Johnson convinced his brothers to work with him to find a way to produce sterile bandages. They went along with his idea, and as a result, the company we now know as Johnson and Johnson was born.[6] Borden and the Johnsons are not alone, for missions seldom develop apart from passion.

Finally, let your life take note of the move of God over the face of its waters. Draw from past experiences and circumstances or the ones He'll use in your future to direct you as you seek to invest your life. There was a schoolteacher named Miss Thompson. Every year, when she met her new students, she would say, "Boys and girls, I love you all the same. I have no favorites."

Teachers don't always tell the truth.

Teddy Stallard was a student Miss Thompson did not like. He wasn't interested in school. He had a blank expression on his face; his eyes had a glassy, unfocused appearance. Whenever she tried to talk to Teddy, he answered in monosyllables. His clothes were dirty, and his hair was never combed. Teddy Stallard was neither attractive nor likeable.

So whenever Miss Thompson marked Teddy's papers, she got a certain perverse pleasure out of putting "X's" next to wrong answers, and when she put "F's" at the top of the papers, she did it with a flair. She should have known better; she had Teddy's records:

First Grade: *Teddy shows promise with his work and attitude, but poor home situation.*

Second Grade: *Teddy could do better. His mother is seriously ill. He receives little help at home.*

Third Grade: *Teddy is a good boy, but too serious. He is a slow learner. His mother died this year.*

Fourth Grade: *Teddy is very slow, but well behaved. His father shows no interest.*

Christmas came, and the boys and girls in Miss Thompson's class brought her Christmas presents. They piled their presents on her desk and watched her open them. One was from Teddy Stallard. She was surprised that he had even bothered. It was wrapped in brown paper and held together with Scotch tape. On the paper were the simple words: "For Miss Thompson, from Teddy." When she opened Teddy's present, out fell a gaudy rhinestone bracelet, with half the stones missing, and a bottle of cheap perfume. The other boys and girls began to laugh at Teddy's gifts, but Miss Thompson at least had enough sense to silence them by immediately putting on the bracelet and dabbing some perfume on her wrist. Holding her wrist up, she said, "Doesn't it smell lovely?" They agreed that it did.

At the end of the day, when school was over and the other children had left, Teddy stayed behind. He slowly came up to his teacher's desk and said softly, "Miss Thompson . . . Miss Thompson, you smell just like my mother . . . and her bracelet looks really pretty on you too. I'm glad you liked my presents."

When Teddy left, Miss Thompson got down on her knees and asked God to forgive her. The next day when the children came to school, they were welcomed by a new teacher. Miss Thompson had become a different person. She had discovered a new sense of mission for her life. She was no longer just a teacher; she had become an agent of God. She was now a person committed to loving her children and doing things for them that would live on long after she was gone. She determined to help all the children, but especially the slow ones—*and especially Teddy Stallard.* By the end of that school year, Teddy showed dramatic improvement. He had caught up with most of the students and was even ahead of some.

She didn't hear from Teddy for a long time. Then one day she received a note that read:

> Dear Miss Thompson:
> I wanted you to be the first to know. I will be graduating second in my high-school class.
>
> > Love,
> > Teddy Stallard

Four years later, another note came:

> Dear Miss Thompson:
> They just told me I will be graduating first in my college class. I wanted you to be the first to know. The university has not been easy, but I liked it.
>
> > Love,
> > Teddy Stallard

And four years later:

> Dear Miss Thompson:
> As of today, I am Theodore Stallard, M.D. How about that? I wanted you to be the first to know. I am getting married next month, the 27th to be exact. I want you to come and sit where my mother would sit if she were alive. You are the only family I have now; Dad died last year.
> Love,
Teddy Stallard

Miss Thompson went to that wedding and sat where Teddy's mother would have sat. She deserved to sit there. Boys like Teddy had become her mission.[7]

A Case Study

So how do you develop your life mission? Draw together your fourfold foundational purpose, values, strengths, abilities, gifts, and passions, along with the activity of God as He leads you through various experiences. Draw these areas together into a singular focus. And if that focus is not readily apparent, then simply go to God in prayer and ask that He *help* you pull them all together into a sense of life mission. Warning: Your life mission won't come to you overnight—it might even take years. We want to know immediately—like by the end of this chapter! Unfortunately, discovering your life mission seldom works that way. But here's the good news: *Nobody wants you to nail this down and start pursuing it more than God.*

It might be helpful to walk through something of a case study on how this can develop, so let me share a bit from my own journey. My clearest first sense of what I wanted my life to be like came in 1978. As mentioned, while I was in Colorado working on a project for one of my father's companies, I saw the second installment of the initial Star Wars trilogy, *The Empire Strikes Back.* It became clear to me that I wanted to have something of that movie's spirit in my life—a sense of being on the front lines of good and evil, caught up in the sweep of history, and making a difference. And, as earlier mentioned, it came to me that this was the invitation of God on every human life.

A few years later, I committed myself to God's basic purposes for every person's life: to know Him and to love Him, to let Him shape my life more and more like Christ, to use what God gave me in order to help others, and to tell others about Him. Once I began the journey of directing my life by those four basic purposes, I found that my values got firmed up pretty quickly as well: values related to my marriage, my role as a parent, and the church.

Now at that time I didn't know a whole lot about spiritual gifts. I *did* know that ever since I was a kid, I was always something of a natural leader. My leadership wasn't always directed in the most positive way, like creating a small-scale rebellion against a teacher in the sixth grade, but the inclination was clearly there. I was also able to communicate in a fairly effective way, winning writing and speaking contests throughout my school years. But now that came into focus. I began to notice how over and over again God seemed to use me in those two areas: leadership and communication.

What was hardest for me to sort through were my passions, because I was passionate about an awful lot of stuff. Sometimes it seemed as if I had ten thousand interests; it still does! But over time, it became increasingly clear to me that my two central passions in life were ministry, specifically through the local church; and evangelism, trying to communicate and connect with people who were not Christians. Then, around 1990, this all just kind of came together in my thinking. I had given my life to Christ and His purposes, He had given me the gifts of communication and leadership, and my passions centered on ministry and reaching out to those who have been turned off to Christianity. Wouldn't it be great if there could be a church where I could use my gifts of leadership and communication to try to connect with the unchurched and be on the front lines of making a difference for God?

And from that began the vision for the church that I began and lead to this day: Mecklenburg Community Church in Charlotte, North Carolina. But it flowed from a sense of life mission to leverage my communication and leadership gifts for the strengthening of the church and the advancement of the cause of Christ. I wanted to do all I could to assist the church in reaching this world for Christ.

That's a bit of my story, and as best I understand it, my mission. It seems so simple now, and so wonderfully fulfilled through what I do. But it took a lifelong journey of sorting through my gifts, passions, experiences, and values. It will be a journey for you as well. But the journey is worth the effort, because it will lead you to the very dream of God for your life.

MISSION IMPOSSIBLE

Now let me tell you what will undoubtedly happen. You will reflect on a mission, pray for a sense of mission, have the beginning contours of it begin to form in your mind under the leadership and vision of the Holy Spirit, and you will begin to gain a vision of what your life could be about. Then, suddenly, one of two thoughts will enter your mind: You'll either feel it's too much of a mission for a single life to ever consider, or you'll feel that your individual contribution won't make that much of a difference. Sensing that reality has come crashing down around you, you'll move back toward an ordinary life.

Don't do it!

Your mission *will* be impossible. Missions from God, for God, and with God, always have been. Just think about the early church's mission to go into the world and make Christ known. It was *geographically* impossible because a great part of the world hadn't even been discovered at that time. It was *physically* impossible because there were no airplanes or radios, printing presses or television, satellites or Internet. *Numerically* it was impossible; there were only about 120 committed followers of Christ at the end of His life. *Financially* it was impossible; the Jewish historian Josephus says that the combined wealth of all of the disciples at that time was equal to around fifty thousand dollars. *Legally* it was impossible; in most parts of the known world it was against the law to talk about Christ. In every conceivable way, coming at it from any angle you want to choose, what Jesus told His followers to do was a mission that was impossible.[8] Even the early Christians themselves, according to the estimation of Theodore Roszak, were "absolute nobodies, the very scum of the earth . . . a handful of scruffy malcontents."[9]

But they did it. And people are still doing it.

Bill Hybels has been a friend and mentor to me for several years. He is the founding and senior pastor of Willow Creek Community Church outside of Chicago. Willow Creek's mission statement is simply a rewording of the Great Commission Jesus gave the church: to turn irreligious people into fully devoted followers of Christ through the local church. The Harvard Business School, under Dr. Leonard Schlesinger, decided to do a case study on that mission statement. They normally evaluate international corporations, but for the first time in the school's history, they decided to take a look at a church.

On the day that they discussed the case, they invited Bill to come and observe. Bill did, taking a seat in the back to listen. Dr. Schlesinger valued class participation, so he began by turning to a student in the front row. Moving toward her desk, he looked her in the eye and asked, "Okay, what do you think of the one-sentence mission statement of Willow Creek Community Church?"

"Well," she said, "they say they're trying to turn irreligious people into fully devoted followers of Christ."

The professor shook his head, and with the emotion and fervor that makes him such a popular instructor, said, "No! No! No! I didn't ask you what the mission statement *was*. I want to know what you think about it! What's your *visceral reaction?* How do you *feel* about it?"

The young student was clearly flustered but said, "Uh, I don't really come from a religious background. But when they say that they're trying to turn irreligious people into fully devoted followers of Christ, it sounds to me like they're, well . . . like they're trying to turn *atheists* into *missionaries!*" And then, collecting her thoughts, she added, "And frankly, sir, I see that as being one *hell* of a *challenge!*"

The class burst into laughter, and Bill was in the back thinking, *Now that's a new twist.* But inside, something else happened to him. For the first time, he thought, *No wonder it's so hard to do what we're trying to do!*[10] Missions are hard. But the good news is that the mission of your life is not a solo event, but one that will be empowered by the very power and presence of the living God. Because of that, the impossible becomes possible.

And what God wants to do through your life mission will *matter,* regardless of its scope, size, stature, or recognition.

Peter Marshall, who was chaplain of the United States senate for years, used to tell a story about the keeper of the spring, a quiet man who lived in the forest high above an Austrian village along the eastern slopes of the Alps. He had been hired many years before by the town council to clear away the debris from the pools of water up in the mountain crevices that fed the spring that flowed through their community.

And he did. With faithful, silent regularity, he patrolled the hills, removing the leaves and branches and wiping away the silt that would otherwise choke and contaminate the flow of water. By and by, the village became a popular attraction for vacationers. Graceful swans floated along the crystal clear spring, the mill wheels of businesses located near the water turned day and night, farmlands were naturally irrigated, and the view from restaurants became incredibly picturesque.

Years went by. One evening, the town council had its semi-annual meeting. As they reviewed the budget, one man's eye caught the salary being paid to the keeper of the spring. He said, "Who is this old man? Why do we keep him on year after year? No one ever sees him. For all we know, he's not even working. Are we sure we need him anymore?" Then, by a unanimous vote, they decided to end the old man's service.

For several weeks, nothing changed. But by early autumn, the trees began to shed their leaves. Small branches snapped off and fell into the pools, hindering the flow of water. One afternoon someone in the town noticed a slight yellowish-brown tint in the spring. A couple of days later, the water was much darker. The next week, a slimy film covered sections of the water along the banks, and a foul odor came from the contaminated river. Then the mill wheels moved slower, and then some finally ground to a halt. The swans left, and then so did the tourists. Because of the bad water, disease and sickness reached deep into the village.

Quickly, the council called a special meeting. Realizing their error in judgment, they hired back the old keeper of the spring, and within a few weeks the river began to clear up. The wheels started to turn, and new life returned to the little town.[11]

Your mission is your spring to keep, and only you can keep it. It may not be seen by anyone but God, but it *matters*.

CHAPTER SEVEN

Ordering Your World

As late as 1960, we didn't have the technology for manned space travel to the moon. Many didn't think we ever would, believing that such an enterprise was impossible. Then President John F. Kennedy did something that shocked the world. On May 25, 1961, Kennedy declared, "This nation should commit itself to achieving the goal, before this decade is out, of landing a man on the moon and returning him safely to earth."[1] Translation? "Let's *make* it happen." The goal that Kennedy set gave everyone a destination, set budgets, and determined where research would take place. The established purpose of landing a man on the moon and bringing him home brought all of the available resources to bear on a single outcome. There was a clear target. Though no one knew how it was going to happen, the Apollo program was born.

And we all know what happened. On July 20, 1969, the crew of *Apollo 11* landed, and Neil Armstrong became the first human being to step foot on the moon. In Armstrong's immortal words,

"That's one small step for [a] man, one giant leap for mankind."[2] The crowning achievement of human endeavor to that point in history happened for a single reason: A group of people ordered their lives around a purpose.

In the business world, this is called *alignment*—taking an organization's core values and purposes and translating them into the day-in, day-out activities of the organization. From goals to strategies, policies to procedures, budgets to hiring, the *purpose* of the company is directly translated into the *practice* of the company. It's when everything the company does is in light of the purpose it is trying to fulfill. It is alignment, perhaps above any other quality, that marks truly exceptional companies.[3] This principle not only mirrors the most successful programs, such as the Apollo space program, or the best companies, such as General Electric, Hewlett-Packard, and Disney, but the most purposeful *lives*.

There are millions of people who would like to write successful novels like John Grisham. For them, writing would reflect their gifts and abilities, passions and temperament. Yet they never do. Why? Often, it is because they have not ordered their lives *around* such a purpose; no steps have been taken in order to achieve the writing of a book! In the foreword of *A Time to Kill*, Grisham's first novel, he shares that he wrote the book by making up his mind that he wouldn't be one of the ones who just *talked* about writing a book—he was going to *do* it. So he ordered his life around that purpose by committing to write one page a day until the book was finished. That simple decision led him to become one of the most successful authors in recent publishing history. And it started with a single page. Alignment, when applied to the human life, means ordering your life around your purposes. As the purpose-driven apostle Paul would counsel, "Let us strip off anything that slows us down or holds us back, . . . and let us run with patience the particular race that God has set before us" (Heb. 12:1 TLB).

THE DISORDERED LIFE

You might find the idea of ordering your life around your purposes and mission appealing but unrealistic. Just think of the week ahead. If you're like most of us, you will put in forty to fifty hours of work at your job; more if there's a key project going on. You'll have to get your kids ready for school every morning, drop them off, pick them up, and maybe attend a PTA meeting or a parent-teacher conference. After school, you're the taxi service for gymnastics, piano lessons, soccer, and basketball—and you might even have to *stay* for some of them, or even worse, help out! In between school and all of those extracurricular activities lies the quality time you want to give them as a parent. Then, for many of us, there's church, which can include a Sunday morning service, Sunday night service, midweek service, small-group meeting, and ministry investment. There's also the United Way Campaign and the Special Olympics program you committed to helping out with months ago. You have plans on Friday for dinner with friends, with relatives scheduled to come in later on in the month, plus a baby shower to give for one of your friends. You're also taking night classes to finish up your degree.

And don't forget, you need to buy your groceries, drop off your clothes at the dry cleaners, wash your car, mow the lawn, take out the garbage, clean the house, pay your bills, and walk the dog. Then you remember that you're married to somebody, and it might be good to spend some time with your spouse. *And that's just next week!* Depressed yet? It's my life, and it's your life. Sometimes it feels as if life pulls at us from about a hundred different directions. But this is the importance of an ordered life. Without it, we have lives filled with busyness and activity, but not purpose. In his book *Ordering Your Private World,* Gordon MacDonald describes where time tends to flow in a disordered life. He speaks of time that is "unseized," time that isn't aligned with our life purpose. His insights are well worth noting.[4]

First, uncontrolled time tends to be poorly invested. In other words, it can and often does go toward things we're not particularly good at, or toward those areas that aren't the best use of our time. If you catch yourself doing what someone else either can or should do while things that only you can do go untouched, then you're seeing this principle at work. Even more wasteful is time spent on meaningless activities, such as mindless TV.

Second, uncontrolled time tends to come under the influence of dominant, demanding people. If you don't claim your time, someone else will. Unseized time is like taking a twenty-dollar bill out of your wallet, laying it out on the street, and then walking away. If you think you're going to come back in a few hours and still find it there, you're crazy. Uncontrolled time is *unprotected* time—it's vulnerable to someone coming along and taking it, monopolizing it, directing it, and claiming it for their own. People will come into your life and force their agendas and their priorities on to you. The bottom line is that if you don't take charge of your schedule first, you will be at the mercy of other people's schedules.

Third, uncontrolled time tends to surrender to the demands of any and all "emergencies." And make sure you notice that "emergencies" is in quotes, because a bit of sarcasm is intended. I was in an office once where I saw a sign taped to a secretary's desk that said, "A lack of planning on your part does not constitute a crisis on my part." MacDonald, who is a pastor, tells of one Saturday afternoon when the phone rang in his home, and when he answered, the woman's voice on the other end of the line sounded very upset. She said, "I've got to see you right away."

MacDonald's first response was to surrender immediately to her sense of emergency and make arrangements to meet her in ten minutes at his office, even though that Saturday was set aside for preparation for his Sunday responsibilities and some much-needed family time.

But he didn't.

He had come to the conclusion that strong people in his world controlled his time better than he did because he had not taken the initiative to command the time before they got to him. He hadn't set any boundaries, much less enforced them. So this time, he asked a very important question: "What is the reason that we have to visit right now?"

"My marriage is breaking up," she answered.

MacDonald asked, "When did you become aware that it was going to break up?"

She said, "Last Tuesday."

"How long do you think the process of breaking up has been going on?" he asked.

And she said, "Oh, it's been coming for five years."

Then MacDonald said, "Since you've seen this coming for almost five years, and since you knew it was going to happen since last Tuesday, why is it important to visit with me right at this moment? I need to know that."

"Oh, I had some free time this afternoon," she answered, "and just thought it might be a good time to get together with you."

Then he said something that many of us should learn to say, in one form or another, to many people in countless situations: "I can understand why you think you have a serious problem. Now I'm going to be very candid with you. I have to speak three times tomorrow morning, and frankly, my mind is preoccupied with that responsibility. Since you've been living with the situation for several years now, and since you've had several days to think about your situation, I'm going to propose that you call me on Monday morning when we can arrange a time where my mind is in much better shape. I want to be able to give you the utmost in concentration. But that's probably not possible this afternoon. How does that sound?"

She thought it was a terrific idea! So did MacDonald.[5] He determined to meet someone's else's agenda for his life with a clear, direct presentation of the agenda he had set for his *own* life. Not legalistically, not heartlessly, not insensitively, and not rudely—just firmly. Not everyone will respond well to the boundaries you set, but that's okay. You have to protect *yourself* or else you are at the mercy of anyone and everyone.

The final place where MacDonald notes that uncontrolled time tends to flow is toward things that gain people's praise. We all know that there are certain things we can do with our time that will generate applause or get people to like us. It may not be the best thing to do with our time, it may even be killing us left and right, but we are pleasers. So we end up with a calendar full of things that take up huge amounts of time that we have no real business doing. But because people will praise us, appreciate us, thank us, or reward us, we keep on saying yes, scheduling event after event, responsibility after responsibility, creating a schedule that is driven by a desire to please.

One September, a friend asked me to fly out to Los Angeles and lead a conference for pastors. This was in line with my sense of mission, so that wasn't the issue. The problem was that I had already blocked out that particular September because I knew that it was going to be a very busy month, full of commitments that had my plate as full as it needed to be. But in my desire to please, I agreed. So after a major conference at Mecklenburg where I had given eight talks in three days, followed by a full weekend of services, three busy days at the office, and then a midweek service, I hopped on a plane and flew off to California where I was to speak five times in less than twenty-four hours. To make matters worse, the time change meant that it was 10:00 P.M. to my body when the evening session began. Then I hopped on a plane, flew back across the country, and got into Charlotte about an hour before the first of Mecklenburg's three weekend services.

It was terrible time control. I should have never accepted. But the request had come from a friend, and I didn't want to disappoint him. On Friday night, in the middle of the California conference, it hit me what a mistake it was. I called my wife, Susan, and said, "I should have never done this. I ought to be home." And Susan, in her tender, loving, supportive way, said, "Serves you right."

One of the problems is the *guilt* we feel for saying no. But you know what? There's something interesting about guilt. You can *be* guilty and not *feel* guilty; and you can *feel* guilty and not *be* guilty. We *should* feel guilt when we do something wrong, and we *shouldn't* feel it when we don't. Saying no to something good in order to say yes to what is best is not something we should feel guilty about. Life is too short not to manage our lives under its limits in order to fulfill our God-given purposes. Our life purposes must determine our schedules. But how does a life become ordered around its purposes? Consider the following sets of dos and don'ts that flow from everything we've explored throughout this book.

DOS AND DON'TS FROM THE IMPORTANCE OF YOUR PURPOSE

The first set of dos and don'ts are those associated with simply knowing the importance of your purpose. Here it is: *Do* let your life be driven by your purpose, and *don't* let it be driven by activities. Time is precious. Every day you are given twenty-four hours in your time bank. No more, no less. Once it's gone, that's it. You can't save it, and you can't store it away. It's a one-time deal. In fact, when you reach the age of thirty-five, you only have five hundred days left to live as you wish. Let me tell you what I mean. The average person lives to be about seventy, which means if you are in your mid-thirties, you have thirty-five years left. During that time you have to eat, work, sleep, travel, and take showers. After taking care of all of the "necessary" things, you only have the equivalent of about five hundred days left to invest into your life as you choose.[6] That's why there is a prayer in the Bible that says, "Teach us to number our days and recognize how few they are; help us to spend them as we should" (Ps. 90:12 TLB).

Not many people pray that kind of prayer. Our busy schedules deceive us into thinking that activity means purpose or significance. It doesn't. Charles Hummel wrote a classic book called *Tyranny of the Urgent*, where he talked about the difference between the urgent and the important. The urgent, he said, cries out for attention, screaming at us to respond and react instantly. Answer this letter! Return that call! Meet with that person! Urgent, urgent, urgent! But the important things, Hummel noted, are more quiet and less demanding. They whisper for attention rather than scream for it. Urgent things are spending time with God, playing with one of your children, talking with a spouse or a friend, or attending to your emotional health. It's not that the urgent things are bad, or that we should ignore them altogether, it's just that if we don't control our time, the urgent things will just take over. We'll spend all of our time running and reacting and racing, and the important things will get pushed away. MacDonald is right. The time must be seized, else it will become prey to any and every demand.

Now what about your life?

Take out your schedule from the past week and make three columns: one for things that are both important *and* urgent, one for things that are important but not urgent, and one for things that are urgent but not important. Then put all of your meetings, parties, errands, trips, conversations, telephone calls, e-mails, lunches, television shows, and things you dragged your kids to (or they dragged *you* to) under one of those three headings. How does it look? How much of the fast-paced schedule of your life falls into that last category—urgent, but not *important?* Only when we stop doing things that are not important do we create the time and place for things that are.

Thornton Wilder wrote a play called *Our Town.* In that play, a young girl named Emily dies while giving birth. In the afterlife, she is granted one wish, and she chooses to go back and watch herself and her family live out one day—her twelfth birthday.

As she watches that day unfold, she cannot believe what she sees. Neither she nor her family members seem to pay attention to each other. Now that she realizes how precious life is, she gets angry that no one is emotionally involved in each other's life. They're too casual; they don't recognize, as she does from the other side of death, that they will not have this day forever. She cannot bear how infinitely precious time is wasted. Then Emily turns to the audience and asks, "Do any of you ever really live life while you're living it?"

That's a good question. It was for Jesus too. He was passionate about making sure that we don't waste our lives. He said, "Anyone who lets himself be distracted from the work I plan for him is not fit for the Kingdom of God" (Luke 9:62 TLB). Jesus wants to make sure we don't play around with how we spend our lives. Building off of that sentiment, the apostle Paul wrote that we should "Live life . . . with a due sense of responsibility, not as [those] who do not know the meaning of life but as *those who do*. Make the best use of your time" (Eph. 5:15–16 PHILLIPS).

DOS AND DON'TS FROM YOUR VALUES

The second set of dos and don'ts to order your life around are those that come from your values: *Do* associate yourself with those things that reflect your values, and *don't* associate yourself with those things that violate your values. The Bible is very clear on this: "Keep a close watch on all you do and think. Stay true to what is right and God will bless you and use you to help others" (1 Tim. 4:16 TLB).

I heard about a guy in Long Beach, California, who went into a chicken place to get some lunch for himself and the woman with him. By mistake, the manager of the store handed the guy the box that held that day's receipts instead of his box of chicken. The man took the box, went to his car, and drove away. When he opened the box and discovered the money, he got back in the car, drove to the store, and gave the money back to the manager. You can imagine how happy that manager was! As the man started to leave, the manager said, "Hold on! I want to call the newspaper and have them take your picture! You're the most honest guy I know!"

"No, no, really," he said. "Please don't do that."

"No, really!" the manager responded. "I want to!"

"No, really, don't," the man implored.

Puzzled, the manager asked, "Why not?"

"Well," he said, "you see, I'm married, and the woman I'm with isn't my wife. My wife doesn't know anything about the two of us, and I'd like to keep it that way."[7]

That's not ordering your life around your God-given purpose, because that kind of life is not ordered around God's given values. If you want your life to be guided, controlled, and directed by your purpose, your life and your values must be in harmony with each other, consistently, in every area, no matter who is looking.

Several years ago, while working for a denomination, my speaking schedule was particularly intense. Within a single month, I traveled first to Virginia, then I headed off to Oklahoma, Florida, Kentucky, back to Florida, and then on to Missouri. Between those trips, as I came home long enough to check my mail, return messages, and exchange my laundry, my oldest daughter, Rebecca, came up to me with tears in her eyes. I was packing and getting ready to head out the door to catch a plane. She asked, "Daddy, are you going on another trip?" I said,

"Yes, honey, but I'll be sure and bring you a surprise." Buying presents was my way of dealing with it. It was just an extension of the "I'm doing it all for you" excuse.

She said, "I don't want a surprise. I want you."

"But honey, I have to go. It's what I do." And that was true. But what I was *doing* was running headlong into my values. And God never calls anyone to pursue his or her purpose in a way that violates his or her values, much less His.

So there I stood. A little five-year-old girl, tears in her eyes, begging her father who traveled too much to stay home. I wish I could give you one of those fairy-tale endings and say that I cancelled the trip, stayed home, and played with my daughter. But I didn't. I looked at her and said, "Honey, I love you very much, but right now, this is what Daddy has to do." That didn't cut it. All she did was cry and say she didn't want me to go. And she kept on crying while I walked out the door to take some stupid trip that really didn't matter much at all in the scope of a lifetime. I did buy her a surprise. Yet I know, and you know, that she doesn't remember what I bought her. But she would have remembered if I had stayed home. And so would I.

What are you doing right now that is in conflict with your foundational life values? Or, what are you *not* doing? If you say your family is important to you, is that value reflected in your life? If you say that a relationship with God is first in your life, then do you see your schedule reflected in terms of your personal devotions and investment in worship and ministry? Pull out your calendar and do a value check. And the reason I say your calendar is because of one of the hardest truths to face about our lives: We *always* find time to do what is *really* important to us.

DOS AND DON'TS FROM YOUR DNA

The third set of dos and don'ts that you should follow are those that come from your DNA—your desires, nature, and abilities. We all have gifts and abilities given to us by God. We have passions and desires that run deep within our hearts. We have unique personalities, such as being an extrovert or introvert, thinker or feeler. Each one of us has a particular background and set of life experiences. We've learned that each of these factors is important and relates to the purpose of God for our lives. So *do* what you are, and *don't* do what you aren't.

Both parts of that equation are important.

God didn't give you a particular shape for the heck of it. He gave it to you for a purpose. Your gifts (including your entire DNA!) are what God has given to you, and what you do with them is your gift back to God. That's why when the apostle Paul wrote to a young man he was mentoring by the name of Timothy, he said: "Put these abilities to work" (1 Tim. 4:15 TLB). And then in a later letter, he said: "Fan into flame the gift of God, which is in you" (2 Tim. 1:6). If you want to experience a purposeful life, then you will be tenacious about making sure that you are doing what you are.

But that's not all.

Ordering your life around your purpose will lead you to be

equally energetic to avoid doing what you *aren't*. If you're a round peg, you shouldn't try to fit into a square hole. If your primary spiritual gift is leadership, you shouldn't be investing the bulk of your time in a ministry of hospitality. If your passion has to do with children, you shouldn't be working exclusively with adults. If your abilities lean toward the technical side of computers, you shouldn't be in sales. If your personality is that of an extrovert, you shouldn't be in a job that isolates you from people. If your experiences have all led you toward being a lawyer, you shouldn't be a veterinarian. You get the point.

There are a lot of things I wish I could do, but I'm really not designed for those things. I can *fight* my design, or I can *accept* my design, appreciate how God made me, and follow His purpose for my life. This is freeing. As the Bible reminds us, "Let everyone be sure that he is doing his very best, for then he will have the personal satisfaction of work well done, and won't need to compare himself with someone else" (Gal. 6:4 TLB). Doing your best isn't simply a matter of personal effort; it's a matter of doing what you *do* best.

Not only do you need to follow this in your life, you need to make sure that others follow it when it comes to your life. In my own life, there are a lot of things people would like for me to do and to be. Many have nothing to do with my God-given purpose and design, much less my mission. I can bend to their expectations—which doesn't honor God and keeps me from leading a purposeful life—or I can say, "No, I'm not going to let you do that to me." Making the right choice is everything: Do what you are, and don't do what you aren't.

DOS AND DON'TS FROM GOD'S PURPOSES

The fourth set of dos and don'ts has to do with God's foundational purposes for your life. Remember, there are four purposes. First, you were made to know and love God. You were designed to be in a loving, personal relationship with our Creator. The apostle Paul put it best when he wrote these words: "Some of these people have missed the most important thing in life—they don't know God" (1 Tim. 6:21 TLB). Second, God made you to become like Christ. Jesus was sent to show you how to live this thing called life, and God's agenda for you is to turn you into someone as much like Jesus as possible. Third, God made you to use what you've been given, including your gifts and abilities, to help others. The goal of life isn't just to take, but to give. And finally, God made you to tell others about Him. He wants your life to be a message to others about His love.

Those are the four foundational purposes for every human life.

So *do* those things that allow you to participate in God's basic purpose for every human life, and *don't* do anything that would cause you *not* to participate in God's foundational purposes for every human life. If something keeps you from knowing and loving God, hinders you from becoming more and more like Christ, stops you from making your unique contribution to the mission and ministry of the church, or prevents you from telling others about Christ, then *you shouldn't do it*. But whatever *does* allow you to pursue those things should be followed with every fiber of your being.

DOS AND DON'TS FROM YOUR MISSION

The final set of dos and don'ts has to do with your mission. *Do* those things that relate to the mission of your life, and *don't* do things that don't relate to the mission of your life. With great insight, the Bible says, "'Everything is permissible'—but not everything is beneficial. . . . [and] not everything is constructive" (1 Cor. 10:23). We have to learn how to say yes to the best and no to the merely good. That's what's really tough, separating the best from the good. We don't have a problem saying no to the bad. Not many of us lie awake at night anguishing over whether we should commit an act of international terrorism or rob a bank. The tough choices are between the good and the best. There are a number of wonderful things that I get asked to do. When I'm asked, I have to do a quick run-through regarding what my life is all about: my values, my DNA, God's foundational purposes for my life, and my mission.

If it fits, then I say yes. If it doesn't, I say no. This is what the apostle Paul was trying to get across when he said, "I run straight to the goal with purpose in every step" (1 Cor. 9:26 TLB).

Now that can be misunderstood and can even at times seem insensitive to what's going on around you, but it is absolutely crucial. There's an old story about a lighthouse keeper who worked on a rocky stretch of coastline. Once a month he would receive a new supply of oil to keep the light burning so that the ships would be protected as they sailed near the rocky coast. Not being far from shore, he received many visitors. One night a woman from the nearby village begged him for some of his oil to keep her family

123

warm. Another time a father asked for some oil to use in his lamp. Another needed a small amount to lubricate a wheel. Since all the requests seemed legitimate, the lighthouse keeper tried to please everyone and grant all their requests. Toward the end of the month he noticed his supply of oil was very low. Soon it was gone, and the light on the lighthouse went out. That evening, several ships were wrecked and countless numbers of lives were lost. When the authorities investigated, the man was very apologetic. He told them that he was just trying to be helpful with the oil. But to his excuses, their reply was to the point: "You were given oil for one purpose, and one purpose only—to keep that light burning!"[8]

So there are some dos and don'ts that will help you be driven by your life purpose.[9] And all five sets are important. You can't follow one set but ignore the set dealing with God's basic purposes. It takes all five to remain on course. You'll be tempted to say, "Well, a little fudging here and there won't make that big a difference," but this is one of those tests where the answer is "all of the above." Wavering on even a single do or don't could alter the entire trajectory of your life. It's often the smallest of compromises that loses the battle.

One of the most tragic events in European history occurred with King Richard III's defeat at the Battle of Bosworth in 1485, immortalized by Shakespeare's great play, *The Life and Death of King Richard III*. The battle was of critical importance because it would determine who would rule England.

The morning of the battle, Richard sent a groom to make sure his horse was ready, because he wanted to ride at the head of his troops. The blacksmith quickly began to shoe the king's horse, but because he had already prepared the entire army, he didn't have enough nails for all four shoes for the horse. The king couldn't wait. The enemy was advancing, and the king had to ride into battle. So the blacksmith did the best he could with what he had.

The armies met on the field of battle, and the fighting began. Richard rode up and down the field, encouraging and challenging his men. Suddenly, at a critical point, he saw his men falling back. They needed him badly, so he rode as quickly as he could to shore up the troops. As he did, one of his horse's shoes fell off—the one that didn't have enough nails holding it on. The horse stumbled and fell, and King Richard was thrown to the ground. The frightened animal rode away, and Richard saw the battle getting away from him as well.

So he waved his sword in the air and uttered that famous line from Shakespeare's play: "My kingdom for a horse!" But there was no horse for him. His army fell to pieces because he could not get to the heart of the battle. Soon the enemy was upon them, and the battle was lost. And since that time, people have had a saying that you may have heard before, but not have known the story behind it:

For want of a nail, a shoe was lost,
For want of a shoe, a horse was lost,
For want of a horse, a battle was lost,
For want of a battle, a kingdom was lost,
And all for the want of a nail.[10]

CHAPTER EIGHT

Maximizing Your Impact

The end of the nineties was filled with stories about the retirement of Michael Jordan. Jordan is certainly a tremendous athlete, but it was his commitment to personal development that took his natural abilities to the level of success that he achieved. When he started out in basketball, he was a scoring machine. Then Dean Smith, his coach at North Carolina, took him aside, and said, "Son, if you want to go as far as you can, you'll need to work on your defense." So Jordan did, and he went on to become one of the only players to win both the scoring title and the defensive title in a single season. As the years went by, his step slowed a bit and his ability to go to the rim lessened. So he developed a fade-away jump shot that was just about unstoppable. Whatever it took to *be* the best, to *stay* the best, and to make the *most* of his abilities, Jordan would do it.

And that's biblical. As Paul wrote to his young mentor Timothy, "Do not neglect your gift. . . . Be diligent in these matters; give yourself wholly to them, so that everyone may see your progress" (1 Tim. 4:14–15). Whatever God has called you to do and to be needs to be optimally leveraged for maximum impact. So how can you elevate your game? There are five absolutely essential ingredients, beginning with a vital relationship with Christ.

THE VINE AND THE BRANCHES

In John 15, Jesus talks in a straightforward way about the relationship between His power and our *connectedness* to Him. "Remain in me, and I will remain in you," He said (v. 4). He went on to say that we could not bear fruit unless we remained in Him. "Apart from me," Jesus said, "you can do nothing" (v. 5). Jesus wanted us to know that we could go on our own strength, our own power, and our own abilities; but we would miss out on *God's* strength, *God's* power, and *God's* abilities. And that's too much to miss.

A more subtle temptation is to substitute *activity* for God, even along the lines of His purpose for your life, for a *relationship* with God. I've heard this syndrome likened to cut flowers. We try to maintain our life and fruitfulness, but we are cut off from our sustaining roots. We seek power without prayer, dynamism without devotion, abundance from God without abiding in Christ. And as cut flowers, no matter how we might try to maintain our appearance, no matter how much water we add, it's only a matter of time before we wither and die.

This is why God, through the prophet Jeremiah, asks an extremely important question of people who have chosen to come to Him: "Who is he who will devote himself to be close to me?" (Jer. 30:21). Only when a life is in close relation and communion with God can the God-given purposes of that life be truly energized, because we need a vital relationship with God to finish the race that has been given us to run. The Bible clearly tells us that "the eyes of the LORD range throughout the earth to strengthen those whose hearts are fully committed to him" (2 Chron. 16:9). If we want to find and follow our purposes in life, we will need God by our sides—and we'll need to be by His.[1]

A COMMITMENT TO EXCELLENCE

Several years ago, the book *In Search of Excellence* became a nation-wide bestseller, and is considered one of the few classics in the business world. Its authors, Tom Peters and Robert Waterman, set out to take a look at America's best-run companies in order to determine what made them successful. They found eight central qualities in America's growing and profitable companies, but the bottom line was that each and every one had made a singular commitment to one thing—*excellence*.

The idea of giving something your best and that effort resulting in success, is not a principle birthed from the marketplace, but from the very Word of God. The apostle Paul says that "the fire will test the quality of each man's work. . . . So whether you eat or drink or whatever you do, do it all for the glory of God" (1 Cor. 3:13; 10:31). The philosophy for excellence is simple: All we do is *for* God and *to* God, and God deserves our best. Mediocrity does not honor God, nor does it reflect His character. A commitment to God, and to His purpose for our lives, demands a commitment to excellence in all that we do.

The temptation is to rationalize our lives in such a way that no matter what we do, we tell ourselves that it's okay. It's like a story I ran across about the FBI, who went into a town to investigate the work of what appeared to be a sharpshooter. They were amazed to find bull's-eyes drawn all over town, with bullets that had penetrated the exact center of the targets. When they finally found the man who had been doing the shooting, they asked him how he had been able to shoot with such accuracy. His answer was simple. First he shot the bullet, then he drew the bull's-eye around where it had hit.[2]

There are two myths when it comes to the subject of excellence. One is that it has to do with ability, and the second, that it is concerned with perfection. Both are mistaken. Excellence is not about ability, but *attempt*. Also, it's not about perfection, but doing the best you can with what you have been given. One of the most gifted violinists in the nineteenth century was Nicolo Paganini. In a performance before a packed house, playing through a very difficult piece of music with a full orchestra, one of the strings on his violin snapped. Paganini kept playing, improvising time and time again to compensate for the lost string.

Then the unimaginable happened. A *second* string broke. And then a *third!* There Paganini stood with three broken strings hanging from his violin. *But he kept playing.* When he was finished, the audience stood and gave him a well-deserved standing ovation.

Then Paganini motioned them to sit down. *What?*, they thought to themselves. He had made it through the final piece, but surely he wasn't going to keep going, was he? Paganini then held the violin high above his head for everyone to see. He nodded at the conductor to begin the encore. He looked at the audience and said, "Paganini—and one string!"[3]

That's excellence.

A TEAM OF SUPPORTERS

Every year I compete in the *Charlotte Observer* Marathon, a ten-kilometer race that is one of the largest and most celebrated in the country. The first time I ran it was nothing less than an education—*in humility*. As you prepare to start the race, everybody gathers as one huge group. I knew I was in trouble when they asked me how fast I took my miles so they could place me in the proper position in the pack. Some people are eight-minute milers, some nine-, and some, like me, wanted to know where the mile-*an-hour* group lined up. I said, "Well, I've never done this before, and I usually only run two to three miles a day."

They said, "In the back."

The first mile was easy. You're pumped up, you're running with thousands of people, and you feel great. The second mile is called reality. By that time, you can't even see the guys who are *real* runners because they are so far out ahead of you. Your side starts to hurt, and you get completely ungodly thoughts about the old men in their seventies who wave at you as they pass. You tell yourself it's okay, because they're just not *pacing* themselves like you are. Then you see a sign that says "Three miles to go," and you realize that there is nothing left to pace.

My salvation was that when I ran that first race, I didn't run it by myself. I ran it with my wife, who is an excellent runner. Running with another person made all the difference in the world, particularly toward the end. At the fifth-mile mark, when there was only a little over a mile to go, I came very, very close to stopping. Sensing my fatigue, she said, "Come on, don't stop now— we're almost there! Come on, you can do it!"

And I did. But it was because of my teammate. Without her encouragement, I wouldn't have made it. But it wasn't just her. I don't know whether it's unique to Charlotte, or if all races share this element, but there are not only thousands of people running, but countless numbers of people lining the streets, cheering you on! I didn't anticipate the enormous support that I received from people along the route of the race. They made signs that said, "Don't give up!" "You look great!" And my favorite, "Don't worry—you're too young to die!" The entire race, runners were cheered, encouraged, and applauded. This kind of encouragement matters in *every* race, including the race of a purposeful life.

A married couple will tell you the benefit of a Christian counselor. An athlete will talk about the importance of a trainer or a coach. A businessperson will talk about the power of a team. It's true for anyone wanting to live a purposeful life as well. When you start developing strategic relationships that support and enhance the purpose of your life, the impact is phenomenal, beginning with the *challenge* they can bring.[4] When I am around someone who is operating at a higher level than I am spiritually, it makes me want to commit myself more deeply, pay attention to areas I've ignored, and deepen my walk with God. It makes me want to focus my energies in order to maximize my impact. This is the idea behind the Bible's admonition, "As iron sharpens iron, so one man sharpens another" (Prov. 27:17).

A second payoff from a team of supporters is *encouragement.* The Bible says: "Let us consider how we may spur one another on toward love and good deeds. Let us not give up meeting together, as some are in the habit of doing, but let us encourage one another" (Heb. 10:24–25). As I experienced in my first race, we all need people who come along beside us and help us to keep going. A third dynamic that relationships can bring is *accountability.* Having those around us who will challenge us by saying, "Why are you doing that?" as well as encourage us by saying, "I think you need to do this," is crucial.

A final contribution that relationships often bring has to do with *support.* The Bible says, "Two are better than one, because they have a good return for their work: If one falls down, his friend can help him up. But pity the man who falls and has no one to help him up!" (Eccles. 4:9–10). A good friend puts his or her arm around you to help you make it through those times when you doubt you can take another step.

One of the most stirring moments in Olympic history occurred during the 1992 Olympics in Barcelona. A twenty-six-year-old Briton named Derek Redmond was favored to win the 400-meter race. Halfway through the semifinal heat, he collapsed on the track with a torn hamstring. Medical attendants raced to his side, bringing out a stretcher to carry him away. He pushed them all away and struggled to his feet. Weeping, he began to hop and limp his way down the track in a desperate effort to finish the race.

His father was on the sidelines and rushed out to him. He grabbed Derek and said, "Son, you don't have to do this."

Derek said, "Yes, I do."

Then his father said, "Well then, we're going to finish this together." And they did. His father wrapped Derek's arm around his shoulder and helped him hobble to the finish line. Fighting off security men, the son's head sometimes buried in his father's shoulder, they stayed in Derek's lane to the end. The crowd clapped, then stood, then cheered, and then wept as the father and the son finished the race.[5]

How do you build these kinds of folks in your life? Look around your circle of influence and take note of people who would positively impact your purpose in life. Make the effort to talk with them and spend time with them. Let them challenge, encourage, and support you, as you do the same for them.

A DEDICATION TO GROWTH

I hold a Ph.D. in systematic theology and, along with my pastoral duties, serve as an adjunct professor of Christian Theology at a seminary. Impressed? Don't be. My father, who also holds a Ph.D., once told me exactly how I should view my educational accomplishments. One evening, as we were talking about "higher degrees," with a twinkle in his eye, he said, "Jim, you know what B.S. stands for, don't you?" I caught his double meaning about B.S. standing for the Bachelor's of Science degree, as well as . . . well, you know. But I was shocked. Did my dad really know about the other meaning for the initials "B.S."? And if he did, what if I said *I* did? I wanted to say, "Well, heck yeah, Dad. I've known that one for years!" but thought better of it. I played it safe and said, "Well, yes, I *think* I do." Then, with a straight face, he said, "Well, M.S. just stands for more of it, and Ph.D. just stands for 'piled higher and deeper.'" I never forgot those words. I'm not sure if it was because it was one of my father's few forays into being a bit off color, or because I learned something from the humility he carried throughout his life about his own achievements in higher education. Yet no one forged within me the priceless worth of preparation for a calling more than my father.

A purposeful life will only maximize its impact when it has been developed along the lines of its purpose. And the Bible agrees with that dedication to growth, saying, "Observe people who are good at their work—skilled workers are always in demand and admired; they don't take a back seat to anyone" (Prov. 22:29 MSG).

The most provocative indication of the importance of personal development comes from the stories told by Jesus. He told a story of three guys who were taken aside by their employer and given a sum of money to manage for him while he was on an extended sabbatical. One guy got $5,000, another got $2,000, and the third one received $1,000.

The first guy took his money, invested it, and doubled it, going from $5,000 to $10,000. The second guy did the same thing with his $2,000, turning it into $4,000. But the third guy took his $1,000 and did nothing with it—absolutely nothing. He just stuck it in a drawer somewhere. The employer returned, called for his employees, and found out the first man had invested his money and doubled it. Notice what Jesus had the employer say in his story: "Well done, good and faithful servant! You have been faithful with a few things; I will put you in charge of many things. Come and share your master's happiness!" (Matt. 25:21). And then the second guy came forward and heard the same thing. But then the third man, the one who had done nothing with what he had been given, came up and said: "Master, I know you have high standards and hate careless ways, that you demand the best and make no allowances for error. I was afraid I might disappoint you, so I found a good hiding place and secured your money. Here it is, safe and sound down to the last cent" (Matt. 25:24–25 MSG). Notice how the employer in Jesus' story responds:

That's a terrible way to live! It's criminal to live cautiously like that! If you knew I was after the best, why did you do less than the least? The least you could have done would have been to invest the sum with the bankers, where at least I would have gotten a little interest.

Take the thousand and give it to the one who risked the most. And get rid of this "play-it-safe" who won't go out on a limb. (Matt. 25:26–29 MSG)

136

God's purpose for your life is a precious thing. When it's revealed, it should not be squandered or buried. Your life purpose should be developed to its fullest potential. If it's treated with contempt, ignored, or tossed aside, your ability to be used by God will be severely diminished. As legendary college basketball coach Bobby Knight once said, "The will to succeed is important, but I'll tell you what's more important: It's the will to prepare. It's the will to go out there every day training and building those muscles and sharpening those skills."[6]

So when it comes to your purpose, and the mission of your life that flows from that purpose, what would it take to increase your level of proficiency? What seminars, books, tapes, or classes would add to your competence? What programs, experiences, skill development exercises, or activities would enhance your abilities? Basketball great Michael Jordan once made the following comment on his success: "I've always believed that if you put in the work, the results will come. . . . That's why I approached practices the same way I approached games. You can't turn it on and off like a faucet. I couldn't dog it during practice and then, when I needed that extra push late in the game, expect it to be there."[7]

If you want to reach your potential in the area of your God-given purpose, whatever it is, it's worth doing. Some of the most talented singers are never heard. Some of the most gifted writers are never read. Some of the best athletes never make the team. Some of the savviest businesspeople never go to the top of the corporate ladder. And some of the best-intentioned people might not hear God say, "Well done." Why? Because they never developed what God gave them to its fullest potential. Many want the purposes of their lives brought to fruition, but they don't want to pay the price. Even more tragic are those who never think of making an investment in their purposes at *all*.

I read about the CEO of a large holding company that had enormous assets. One day he invited a friend over to his office. As they talked, he proudly pointed out a row of notebooks on his bookshelf that laid out specific plans for each of the company's ventures. The notebooks had mission statements, action plans, and pro formas all neatly typed, categorized, and cross-indexed. Each volume took incredible thought and planning, masterpieces of strategic thinking, blueprints for guaranteed success. Then he told his friend why he wanted to meet. He wanted to develop a better relationship with his wife and kids. There was distance, strain, and difficulty. His friend asked him a simple question: "You obviously do a superb job at planning and setting goals for this company. Have you ever spent some time doing the same sort of thing for your family?"[8]

Many people develop their lives financially, intellectually, physically, emotionally, and even spiritually. But few do it in concert with their life purposes. The words of the apostle Paul ring true: "Do you not know that in a race all the runners run, but only one gets the prize? Run in such a way as to get the prize. Everyone who competes in the games goes into strict training. They do it to get a crown that will not last; but we do it to get a crown that will last forever" (1 Cor. 9:24–26).

A CHANNEL FOR ACTION

A dear friend called me from her home in Tennessee to share a sense of frustration that had been building up within her for several months. She had volunteered to serve as a teacher for a missions program in her church, and through her leadership and gift of teaching, the group had grown from a handful of girls to nearly forty children per week—*half of whom had been previously unchurched!* She found that she could connect with the girls through contemporary Christian music and relevant topics. You would think her church would be *ecstatic!* They weren't.

She was confronted by the person who led the missions department and told that she was not following the denominational program the way it was written. "I know I'm tweaking it a bit, adding a few things here and there, like having an opening song, or having some games and contests," said my friend, "but I'm still getting across the content. I'm just trying to freshen it up a little. I want the girls excited about missions! The way it was, it just wasn't connecting." It fell on deaf ears. She was asked to follow the program with exact specificity or step aside.

As I listened, my heart was breaking. I knew this woman to be a team player. This was not a smoke screen for bucking authority. Here was a woman who loved Christ, demonstrating obvious gifts in evangelism and teaching, and bearing enormous fruit in the context of the local church. Instead of being celebrated, she was being shut down. She was not being allowed to pursue her purpose. Someone should have spotted what was happening, seen the gifts she had, and either allowed her to keep "tweaking" the formula or worked with her in building an outreach ministry for young girls. Neither took place.

Jesus gave some interesting counsel to the very first teams of ministers sent out in His name: "If anyone will not welcome you or listen to your words, shake the dust off your feet when you leave that home or town" (Matt. 10:14). It was a serious thing to reject God's message. It is equally serious for the purpose of a life to be stifled. You simply must find a channel for action in light of the purpose of your life.

A young man in his thirties came to the church I pastor and said, "I want a place where I can invest myself and make a difference." He had gifts in evangelism and marketing, so that's where he was turned loose. To date, he has probably brought more people to Christ than any other single individual in our community of faith. Some time after he came to us, I learned that he had a simple prayer before selecting a church: "God, lead me to a place that will challenge me and let me express the purpose in life You have for me."

PERSISTENCE TO THE END

I've never been one for the collection of inspirational quotes or motivational sayings. I've always been motivated by *stories*. But when I was a boy, I came across something that former President Calvin Coolidge once said, and it has stuck with me my entire life.

Here it is:

> Nothing in the world can take [the] place of persistence. Talent will not; nothing is more common than unsuccessful individuals with talent. Genius will not; unrewarded genius is almost a proverb. Education will not; the world is full of educated derelicts. Persistence and determination alone are omnipotent.

This idea certainly wasn't original with Coolidge. The Holy Spirit inspired the apostle Paul in a similar fashion in his first letter to the church at Corinth, writing, "Therefore, my dear brothers, stand firm. Let nothing move you. Always give yourselves fully to the work of the Lord, because you know that your labor in the Lord is not in vain" (1 Cor. 15:58). Persistence and determination are decisive.

The National Sales Executive Association released some interesting statistics. They found that 80 percent of all new sales are made after the fifth call to the same prospect, but that almost half of all salespersons make one call and then cross off the prospect. Twenty-five percent quit if the second call isn't productive. Another 12 percent give it a third try but then stop. Only 10 percent keep at it until they succeed.[9] Many fail to maximize their potential in life because they fail to pursue their purposes with steadfast, relentless commitment.

Just ask Lynn Brooks. In October 1998, she competed in her

nineteenth Hawaiian Open Ironman Triathlon, a grueling competition that involves a swim in the open ocean of more than two miles, followed by more than one hundred miles of biking, and ending with a full marathon run. Featured in an NBC-TV program on the event, Brooks shared how one year, during the marathon leg of the competition, she left the race and entered an aid tent. With her body aching and her emotions drained, the desire to stop was overpowering. In the tent, sitting on a bench and drinking an ice-cold beer, was a man who was relaxing. Reading her thoughts, he said, "All you have to do is drop out of the race like me." Suddenly, she said that she realized he represented the devil. She left the aid tent and reentered the race. Reflecting on the moment filled her eyes with tears. "It was the hardest, and most glorious, day of my life."[10]

This lesson cannot be understated. Living a life of purpose, one that makes a difference and maximizes its impact, will demand persistence and determination. It may be the single most important message that can be heard. After the heroic days of World War II, when life had slowed down a bit for Winston Churchill, the great leader was asked to speak at Sandhurst, his alma mater. To the audience of schoolboys, he said, "Young men, be sure you take copious notes, because this will probably be one of the greatest speeches you'll ever hear." He then situated himself behind the podium, and said, "Never give up."

After a minute's silence, with even more conviction, he said it again: "NEVER give up!"

Then came another lengthy pause, after which Churchill

pounded his fist on the podium, and shouted at the top of his lungs: "Never, never, never, never, NEVER GIVE UP!"

And then he turned and sat down.[11]

An Audience of One

There was a young man who played on the football team of Columbia University. He was good enough to make the team, but not good enough to start or even to play very much. But he impressed his coach and his teammates with his enthusiasm and also with the way he loved and cared for his father. Whenever his father would visit, the boy and his father would walk around the campus, arm in arm, in intimate conversation.

One day the coach received word that the boy's father had died. When he told him, he said, "Now son, if there is anything I can do for you—anything—you just let me know, and I'll do it." The boy surprised him by saying, "Then let me start in Saturday's game." The coach thought to himself, He's not good enough! But he had promised, so he thought he'd leave him in for a few plays and then take him out.

The day of the big game arrived. On the very first play, the boy whose father had died single-handedly made a tackle that threw the opposing team for a loss. Play after play, that kid played football like you wouldn't believe. The coach left him in for the entire game. He was voted the outstanding player of the game.

When the game was over, the coach said, "Son, what got into you today?"

"Do you remember when my father would visit me here, and we would walk arm in arm around the campus?" the boy said. "My father and I shared a secret that nobody here knew. You see, my father was blind, and today was the first time he ever saw me play."[12]

There was a Latin phrase used during the time of the Reformation that spoke of living life *coram deo,* before the heart of God. Every day, God watches you play. He's waiting and watching to see what you will do with all that He's given you. Give it your best.

CHAPTER NINE

Following God's Lead

I f only I knew the exact will of God for my life, I'd do it. No questions asked. But I don't know it!"

Ever said that? Or felt it? One of the greatest mistakes that we could make would be to gain a sense of purpose for our lives, develop a sense of mission, and then pursue it apart from the active leadership and direction of God. But following God's lead, or what is commonly called "discovering God's will," is often written off as virtually impossible. So let's see if we can grasp this thing called the will of God so that we can take our purposes and put them under God's daily leadership and direction.

UNDERSTANDING GOD'S WILL FOR YOUR LIFE

The Bible talks about God's will for your life in three ways. First, it talks about God's *ultimate* will for your life. We talked about this in chapter 3 under the idea of God's four foundational purposes for your life—to know and to love God, to become more like Christ, to serve with your gifts and abilities, and to tell others about Christ.

The second major dimension of God's will for your life is His *moral* will. God's moral will has to do with how we should think and believe, what we should value and honor, and from that, how we should live. So many times we skip right past this in trying to figure out what God wants us to do in a given situation—looking for signs, the opening and closing of doors—when God's moral will for our lives is already speaking to what we should or should not do. In fact, I am convinced that the day-in, day-out will of God for our lives is primarily directed through His moral will for our lives.

You may disagree, believing that while God's moral will is easily applied in some areas—such as whether you should lie, cheat, steal, or murder—it's a bit obscure on the more subtle issues of life. Let's say you're trying to decide whether to take a particular job offer. You begin by making an analysis of the offer in terms of money and benefits, whether the position fits your gifts and abilities, and whether you think it's a good company. Let's say all of that looks good. So does God want you to take the job? You're tempted to blow off the question because all the signs look good, and you can't imagine how God's moral will could have anything to do with it. It is, after all, just a job!

But let's dig a little deeper.

Let's say you have a wife and two young children, and the new job would require an enormous amount of travel that would strain your marriage and make you a stranger to your kids. Or the job would rip your wife and kids out of a situation that is integral to their wholeness and happiness. Or maybe the family angle is fine, but the work is in a questionable profession or has ties to some products or companies you're not comfortable with, and your position would directly, or indirectly, make you a supporter of those questionable activities. Or let's say that the job would take you out of a church or a particular ministry where God is using you like crazy. Suddenly what seemed to be dollars and cents, geography and career track, becomes a question of knowing and following God's *moral* will for your life.

Here's a biblical principle that is simply not being advanced enough: *God's will for your life is always, first and foremost, a moral will.* If you're struggling with whether God wants you to do something that goes against His moral will for your life, you can stop struggling. God has already made His will known to you, because His guidance for the day-in, day-out flow of your life is primarily moral.

Now before we get to the last aspect of God's will, it's important to realize that in most situations, God's direction and leadership for your life doesn't go any further than His ultimate will—that you know Him and be in a relationship with Him—and then His moral will. From that, you simply take your abilities, passions, personality, and background and launch out in light of your mission. The Bible gives the impression that once you are in a relationship with God and follow His moral will, the rest is up to you. Within those confines, God may not have a particular preference for what you *do* or *do not, do!* As C. S. Lewis described it, "It is like a play in which the scene and the general outline of the story is fixed by the author, but certain minor details are left for the actors to improvise."[1]

In the Garden of Eden, God was very clear to Adam and Eve: "You are free to eat from any tree in the garden; but you must not eat from the tree of the knowledge of good and evil, for when you eat of it you will surely die" (Gen. 2:16–17). That was God's moral will, but also the freedom He gave for choice. Play it out. You can imagine that when Adam got hungry, turned to Eve, and said, "I think we should eat," she said, "Why don't you go out and get some fruit, and I'll fix it up." So Adam went out, got some fruit, gave it to Eve, and sat back and waited for dinner.

Then Eve said, "Hey Adam, which of these fruits do you want me to fix? I want to follow God's will, but I'm not sure what He wants me to do. Would you go ask Him what I should do for supper?" So Adam goes out to talk to God but then comes back in a few minutes. Eve says, "What does God want us to do?" And Adam says, "Well, He didn't really say."

"What do you mean He didn't say?"

"He didn't say! He just repeated what He told us before: that we could eat from any tree of the garden except from the tree of the knowledge of good and evil."

So Eve goes, "Did any of this fruit come from there?"

Adam said, "Nope, not a one."

"So what should I make?"

"Well," ventures Adam, "let's start off with cherries."

So they do. But then Eve says, "How should I fix them? Should I slice them, dice them, mash them, bake them in a pie, make them into a cobbler, or just pull together a fruit salad? I don't want to do anything displeasing to God. Be a sweetheart and go back one more time to ask Him." So he goes back to God, comes back, and Eve says, "What did He say?" And Adam says, "Same thing. From any tree we may eat freely, but from the tree of the knowledge of good and evil, you shall not eat."

Then it clicked. That one moral law covered the will of God for their lives. As long as they didn't get any fruit from that one tree, they couldn't miss doing what God wanted![2]

Now let's go back to our job illustration. Let's say that under God's moral leadership, you determine that whatever job you take must honor your basic gifts and passions, protect your family life, keep you in the city in which you now live for the sake of a particular ministry investment you're making, and be with a business that has integrity. Each of these requirements has been established in light of your understanding of not only God's purpose for your life, but His moral will. Once those issues are covered, there might be hundreds of jobs that would make the cut. It would be a mistake to assume automatically that God has one and only one company out there for you to join. His will may not go past the moral level.

Let's apply this to marriage. The Bible doesn't say you have to get married. Nowhere in the Bible does it teach that there is one and only one Mr. or Ms. Right out there for you. The Bible only talks about *moral* dynamics as to whom you should marry. There might be any number of people out there whom you could marry and God would be more than willing to bless. We all want God's leadership and will to be specifically detailed like a road map. "Go here," "Do this," "Take that job," "Marry that person." Yet nine times out of ten, what God gives us is more along the lines of a compass.

Having said that, the Bible does speak to a third "will"—the specific will of God for our lives that leads us in unique, direct ways. While God's will for our lives is primarily moral, and that moral will guides the bulk of our day-in, day-out decisions, there is still an individual will that reflects God's unique hand on your life. There may very well be places He wants you to go, things He wants you to do, or a person He wants you to marry. But remember! God's *specific* will for your life will *never* contradict God's *moral* will for your life. If those two are in conflict, you have misread God's specific will. If you feel God is telling you to do something that is clearly condemned in the Bible, you can rest assured that it isn't God who is talking to you.

But here's the good news: God doesn't want this to be a guessing game! He wants to guide us! We often talk about "discovering" the will of God, trying to "find out" where God is leading, as if we're looking for the answer to a mystery. That's not true. God *wants* us to know His will. He *wants* us to recognize His leadership. Notice what God said through the prophet Isaiah: "The LORD says to his people, . . . [you] will be led by one who loves [you]" (Isa. 49:8, 10 TEV). And in the Psalms, God says: "I will instruct you and teach you in the way which you should go; I will counsel you with My eye upon you" (Ps. 32:8 NASB).

God is very concerned about your knowing and being in His will. Do you know what that means? It means that you can be free from the fear that God may not give you the information you need to decide within His will. It means that you can be released from the fear that God's will is a deep, dark mystery that you may never be able to understand. It means that you can be free from the fear that finding God's will depends solely on you and that you might miss out on God's will because you weren't able to see it.[3] God wants you to know His will. He wants to guide you. So what are the practical dynamics for tapping into His will? Begin with simply listening to His voice.

HEARING A WORD FROM GOD

Hearing a word from God sounds impossible, doesn't it? Yet if Christianity is true, then there really is a God on the loose Who wants to know us and be known by us. So how do we hear His word to our life?

The first way God speaks to us is through His written Word, the Bible. The Bible is not some kind of magical book when it comes to revealing the will of God, where you blindly open it up, place your finger on a random verse, and take it as God's guidance. Paul Little wrote about a guy who did that, wanting to hear a word from God, and it didn't quite turn out the way he wanted. He took his Bible, stuck his finger on a page, and read "Judas went out and hanged himself." That didn't make him feel very good, so he tried again for more explanation. This time his finger landed on the phrase, "Go thou and do likewise." Now he was really worried. Surely this couldn't be God's message! So he did it a third time. His finger landed on a verse that said, "And what thou doest, do quickly."[4]

That's not how the Bible plays into God's will for your life. Listen instead to how the apostle Paul described the Bible: "The whole Bible was given to us by inspiration from God and is useful to teach us what is true and to make us realize what is wrong in our lives; it straightens us out and helps us do what is right. It is God's way of making us well prepared at every point" (2 Tim. 3:16–17 TLB). Let's say you're married, and you're struggling with a particular sexual issue, such as having an affair. You're wondering whether God would have you pursue an intimate relationship with someone other than your spouse. It's appealing to you, but you aren't sure and want to know God's will on the matter. So you go to the Bible and read this passage in Hebrews: "Honor marriage, and guard the sacredness of sexual intimacy between wife and husband. God draws a firm line against casual and illicit sex" (Heb. 13:4 MSG). Now that's pretty clear, isn't it? So there's your direction. Through His Word, God has addressed thousands upon thousands of situations, circumstances, and decisions. This is what David meant when he said to God, "Your word is a lamp to my feet and a light for my path" (Ps. 119:105). Now we may struggle with whether we are going to *follow* what He has said to us, but because we have the Bible, trying to figure out *what* He wants us to do isn't usually the problem.

The second way God talks to us is through prayer. Prayer is not simply talking *at* God; it is a conversation *with* God. When we pray, God takes part in the conversation by speaking to us regularly and directly. God doesn't usually speak through an audible voice—although He could. He tends to speak to us in a still, small voice that we sense in our spirits. Prayer focuses our thoughts on God. And when we pause during our prayer time to listen to God's response, we come in tune with all that He is and all that He might want to say to us. Or as one writer in the Bible put it, "I pray . . . and wait for what he'll say and do" (Ps. 130:6 MSG).

When I quiet myself and begin to pray, I gain an insight into life that comes at no other time and in no other way. I am often convinced of God's leading and direction. Sometimes it's simply a sense of peace about a particular choice or decision. Why? Because prayer opens our inner world to the voice of God. It's when we pay attention to Him and let Him have the floor. I've been in prayer and felt the need to make a phone call, write someone a note, give a financial gift, stop and help somebody on the side of the road, cancel a day's schedule and spend some time with my wife or kids, or do something radically differently than I had planned. When I have followed through on those promptings from God through the Holy Spirit, it's amazing what I've experienced. Somebody will say, "You know, I'm really glad you called. You'll never know how much I needed that." Or I'll hear, "You know, that note you sent me came at just the right time." Even more exciting are those blazing insights you'll receive in regard to a decision, a course of action, or a way of life.

Again, God will *never* prompt you—even through prayer—to do anything that goes against Scripture. Promptings, and even feeling a peace about something, are subjective feelings and can be very misleading. If you think you're feeling a prompting to do something that goes against Scripture, you can rest assured that it isn't an authentic prompting. You may have heard about, or even read, Neale Donald Walsch's series of books called *Conversations with God.* According to Walsch, God has talked to him and writes through him to our world. Walsch's books have been huge best-sellers. But what Walsch *claims* God said to him often goes against what God *has* said in the Bible. Now either God is very confused and doesn't have a clue where He stands, or Walsch hasn't had the conversations with God he thinks he's had! Remember, whatever you think comes to you through prayer should be checked by Scripture.

But keep praying. I'll never forget reading a challenge from a man named Norton Sterret. It was from an address back in 1948 to a group of college students. All he said was: "How many of you who are so interested in finding out the will of God for your life spend even five minutes a day praying for Him to show it to you?"[5] Convicting, isn't it? It's a good challenge, because prayer is one of the ways God talks to us. And missing it would be so tragic. One of the most poignant verses in all of Scripture is recorded by the author of Proverbs, where God says: "If only you had listened . . . I would have told you what's in my heart; I would have told you what I am thinking. I called, but you refused to listen" (Prov. 1:23–24 NCV).

THE THREE "C's"

But what do you do when you are trying to discern God's will for your life, and nothing seems to come to you through the Bible or through prayer? Are there some *indirect* ways God can use to lead us and make His will known? Yes, through what I'll just call the three "C's": circumstances, common sense, and counsel. Let's begin with circumstances.

It's like praying, "God, if you want me to take this job, have them call me by ten o'clock this morning." They call, so you see it as a sign from God. Or maybe you run into an old high school flame, by chance, and it's been years since you've seen or heard from that person. And wouldn't you know, you're both single and living in the same city. Must be fate! You automatically think of romance, even marriage. Or you're wondering whether you should move into a new house, and then the next day, you drive by a home you've driven by a hundred times—and it's always been your dream house—and see a "For Sale" sign out front! You think, *I must be supposed to buy it and move!* I read of one woman who was trying to decide whether to take a trip. She had the time and the money, but she didn't know what God's will might be. She tossed and turned all night, and when she woke up, she noticed that her digital clock said that it was 7:47 in the morning. She called the airline, and sure enough, the flight she would take would be on a 747, so she decided it must be God's will.[6]

Ever played life this way? I have. Many times, it's a legitimate thing to do. God can work through circumstances, open and close doors, create opportunities, and then place it all in our paths in order to direct our steps or confirm a particular direction. Circumstances can entice us to move forward, check something out, or explore something new; and when that first, tentative step is met by *another* encouragement, *another* open door, *another* confirmation, we feel compelled to move further and further. It's exciting! We look back and see a trail of events where God clearly led us, step by step, toward a particular choice. Countless times I have prayed, "God, please, as best as I know, this is the path I am to take. If it's not, close the door, or send me a red flag that will help me know that I'm off course. Everything seems to point toward moving ahead, so I am, but if this is something You don't want me to do, please let me know. Prompt those around me to see what I can't see, bring some aspect of this to light that I may not be thinking about."

But that kind of prayer is very different than setting up some kind of experiment or test for God where He is supposed to jump in a box and perform through circumstances. Like, "God, if you want me to do this, have the phone ring . . . NOW! Okay, didn't ring, so I'm off the hook." That's making God a joke, or into some kind of cosmic bellhop. No, this is about giving God permission to act, asking for His guidance.

So here's what else I'll pray. "God, help me to be discerning about what I see and hear so that I can truly sense Your leading." That prayer is important, because there are a lot of open doors that God never opened; *we did.* And there are many coincidences that are just that—*coincidences.* Not every need, much less every opportunity, that comes our way is an invitation from God.

One more thing. Not only do we have to be careful about saying what is God, and what is us, but when it comes to circumstances, we also have to ask ourselves once again if God's moral will, as revealed in the Bible, has already spoken. And because of that, the circumstances, no matter how unique, are not even *meant* to be considered. Now that's huge, because remember: God will never lead you to do anything that violates His moral will, and sometimes we can feel circumstances should overrule everything. Not so.

About this time, some of you might be saying, "You don't understand. My situation is so clear, so unique, and everything came together in such a compelling way! I know the Bible says one thing, but let me just walk you through all that's happened!" Sorry, but I wouldn't buy it, and neither should you. Scripture reminds us of the reality that there really is a being called Satan who is alive and well on planet Earth. And if you don't think Satan can orchestrate a few circumstances to lead you down the wrong path, you've underestimated him. If God's moral will has spoken to your situation, it takes precedent over the circumstances—no matter *what* they are.

This leads us to the second "C": *common sense.* Along with circumstances, this is one of the main ways that we make decisions. We run through a mental checklist of pros and cons, strengths and weaknesses, pluses and minuses, and see what comes out on top. This can be a good thing, something that the Bible smiles on, because it was God who gave us our common sense. He gave it to us for a reason—to use it! That's why the apostle Paul once wrote the following words to a group of Christians: "For this reason, since the day we heard about you, we have not stopped praying for you and asking God to fill you with the knowledge of his will through all spiritual wisdom and understanding" (Col. 1:9).

But just as there are dangers in following circumstances uncritically, there can be dangers in making our decisions on the basis of reason alone. The first is that our reasoning is not always objective. British historian Paul Johnson authored an interesting book called *Intellectuals.* In that work he chronicled the lives and philosophies of such great minds as Jean-Jacques Rousseau, Karl Marx, Bertrand Russell, and Jean-Paul Sartre, each noted around the world as a towering intellect. But here's what Johnson found. For most of them, their philosophies were not based on noble convictions, but on the choices they had made in their own lives. For example, the eighteenth-century French philosopher Jean-Jacques Rousseau had five children out of wedlock and abandoned them all. Then he wrote, supposedly out of his reasoning and intellect, that children do not need parents to give them discipline or guidance; the state should be responsible for raising them. This idea is shaping educational and child-rearing theories to this day. The conclusions he had supposedly reached through reasoning were actually influenced by his desire to justify the moral choices he had already made. His reasoning wasn't objective. He had an agenda, and it colored his thinking. It can color ours too.[7]

That's not the only problem with operating by reason alone. Reason, by itself, leaves out faith. God may call you to do the unreasonable. In fact, He often specializes in it. Here's the Bible's definition of faith: "Now faith is being sure of what we hope for and certain of what we do not see" (Heb. 11:1). I know that when God led me to follow Him in regard to planting Mecklenburg Community Church, it went completely against common sense. To drop everything and go out and start a new church—no people, no money, no building, nothing—it was crazy! But it was what God asked me to do, and I'm *so glad* I followed. This is what the apostle Paul was after when he wrote the following verse to the church at Corinth: "For the foolishness of God is wiser than man's wisdom, and the weakness of God is stronger than man's strength" (1 Cor. 1:25).

Reason, by itself, is limited in how far it can direct you in regard to God's perfect will for your life. It can't always lead you to the deepest of truths about life and how it should be lived, because God's ways are bigger and God's wisdom is deeper than our common sense. If all we have is our own wisdom, we are unable to be truly wise, because God's wisdom, even when it seems foolish, is where true wisdom is found.

This brings us to our third and final "C": *counsel.* Advice from godly people is seldom sought but highly regarded in the Bible. Take a look at this sampling from just one book of the Bible, the Book of Proverbs:

> The way of a fool seems right to him, but a wise man listens to advice. (Prov. 12:15)

> Plans fail for lack of counsel, but with many advisers they succeed. (Prov. 15:22)

Listen to advice and accept instruction, and in the end you will be wise. (Prov. 19:20)

Make plans by seeking advice. (Prov. 20:18)

I am shocked at how many people attempt to make life-changing decisions, try to determine God's will for their lives, or seek to follow their life purposes, and *never* bring other people into the process! This causes you to miss out on two very important tools that God wants to use in guiding you, the first being *objectivity*. You're not objective about yourself, much less your life. Neither am I. I'm surrounded by my emotions, my circumstances, my biases, and my desires. I need to go to people who can see things independently of all that. But that's not all I get through counsel. I also get *wisdom*. When I go to someone else, I get his or her experiences, maturity, and knowledge concerning what I'm trying to decide. This isn't about running your life by committee, or taking what somebody says and feeling as if you have to follow it. It certainly shouldn't be used as a shortcut to the hard work of studying the Bible for God's moral will, or investing in prayer, evaluating circumstances, and using your common sense. But going to someone who is intimate with God, intimate with you, and able to tell you what you may not want to hear, is invaluable.

Don't be like the schoolteacher who lost her life savings in a business scheme that had been elaborately set up by a swindler. When she lost her investment, she went to the Better Business Bureau. The official heard her story and then asked, "Why on earth didn't you come to us first?" Her reply? "I was afraid you'd tell me not to do it."[8]

A Lesson from a Very Old Man

We all want to know where we're going before we leave. But a final truth about the leadership of God is that He has a tendency to reveal His will to us *as* we follow Him. It's as we follow His leading that we find the next step. No one passed this on to the world more clearly than an old man named Abram. Take a look at how the Bible records how God led him: "The LORD . . . said to Abram, 'Leave your country, your people and your father's household and go to the land I will show you. I will make you into a great nation and I will bless you; I will make your name great'" (Gen. 12:1–2).

God made His will known to Abram: Leave where you are, leave all that you have, and go, and I will make you into a great nation and make your name great. Sounds good, right? But did you notice what God left out? *Where he was to go!* All God said was go to a place that He would show. You can just imagine Abram saying, "So God, let me get this right. You want me to go?"

And God says, "Right."

"Just *go?* That's *it?* Not even a north, south, east or west—just . . . *go?*"

And God said, "Yep. You go, and I'll show the way."

We don't often think of God's will coming that way. But more often than not, that is exactly the way He will operate. God's will seldom comes in a final, finished package where everything is laid out for you from start to finish. What usually happens is that God's will for your life will come bit by bit, step by step, unfolding in its fullness as you follow Him in obedience and trust.

But that's not all. God also has a tendency to reveal His will to us to the *degree* that we have followed His will *up to that point*. Take a look at what happened next to Abram:

> So Abram left, as the LORD had told him. . . . And they set out for the land of Canaan, and they arrived there. Abram traveled through the land. . . . The LORD appeared to Abram and said, "To your offspring I will give this land. . . . Lift up your eyes from where you are and look north and south, east and west. All the land that you see I will give to you and your offspring forever. . . . Go, walk through the length and breadth of the land, for I am giving it to you." (Gen. 12:4–7; 13:14–15, 17)

When Abram followed what he *knew* of God's will, God gave him even *more* knowledge of His will. God reveals Himself to those who not only want to know His will, but who will act on it. The more we obey, the more He reveals!

But even that's not the final lesson from our old friend. Through Abram's life we learn that the fullness of God's will for our lives is often only revealed to us at the *end* of our *following!* Only when we complete our following do we bring His will to life and see all that He intended. Take a look at what God had in mind for Abram all along:

> When Abram was ninety-nine years old, the LORD appeared to him and said, . . . "You will be the father of

many nations. No longer will you be called Abram; your name will be Abraham, for I have made you a father of many nations. . . . I will establish my covenant as an everlasting covenant between me and you and your descendants after you for the generations to come, to be your God and the God of your descendants after you." (Gen. 17:1, 4–5, 7)

Here we find God's full plan for the life of Abram, now Abraham, come into view. Through Abraham, the Jewish people's relationship with God began. God called them into a community, which would become known as Israel, a new community that would introduce to the world the idea of a relationship with God through faith and point the way toward the universal new community which would one day be called the *church*, founded by a descendant of Abraham by the name of Jesus. That's a lot from a single step of obedience. This is why *following* the will of God is so important to *seeing* the will of God. It's like taking an acorn, planting it, and letting it grow into a mighty oak tree. Obedience is planting the seed God has given to you to act on and letting it grow into hundreds and hundreds of limbs and branches. *But it takes the planting.* Just like knowing the fullness of the will of God for your life takes the *following.*

When the mapmakers of the Middle Ages came to the end of the world as they knew it, having exhausted the extent of their geographical knowledge, they wrote an interesting phrase on their maps: "Beware: Dragons Lurk Beyond Here," or as historical novelist Sharon Kay Penman titled one of her novels set in the medieval era, *Here Be Dragons*. At the edges of our knowledge of the map of God's leadership, we need not fear dragons. Instead, the lettering should read, "Here Begins Faith."

Chapter Ten

Becoming a Maker of History

When I played basketball, nothing was worse than sitting on the bench. I would sit on the sidelines, watching the other players, wanting more than anything to be out on the court as part of the action. I'd keep looking down the bench toward the coach, trying to catch his eye, hoping he'd put me in the game. I wanted to be used! Don't we all feel that way? We want to make a difference; we want to be part of the action, to give our lives to something that will matter—not just sitting on the sidelines watching others play.

In the deepest parts of our hearts, we all want to be makers of history.

This book has tried to explore how to experience a purposeful life, and the final component is letting your purpose in life be used by God on the front lines of His advancing kingdom. Few have modeled this for all of time and history more effectively than a young woman named Esther. From a defining moment in her life, we'll be able to discover four steps that are absolutely essential if you want to become a person who allows your purpose in life to make history.

Esther was a Jewish woman living in Persia, a descendant of those Jews who had been carried away into exile from Jerusalem by Nebuchadnezzar, king of Babylon. Both of Esther's parents died when she was only a child. She was raised by her cousin, Mordecai, who was a very godly man. He loved Esther and raised her as he would his own daughter. Esther grew to be a beautiful woman, both inside and out. She was so beautiful, in fact, that when the king of Persia searched the land for a wife, no one was found to be fairer than Esther. As a result, she was selected to be the queen, though no one in the king's palace suspected that she was a Jew.

Then an evil man named Haman appeared on the scene, gaining the king's confidence. He had such a high position in the government that the king commanded all of the royal officials to bow down to Haman wherever he traveled. And everyone did—except Mordecai, who would only bow down to God. This infuriated Haman, insulting his pride, which led him to devise a plot not only to kill Mordecai, but also to wipe out the entire Jewish race. He started a campaign to deceive the king into believing all kinds of horrible things about the Jews who were living in his kingdom. Once he had the king worked up, he convinced him to sign an edict that would award large amounts of money to anyone who killed a Jew. Haman knew that if people could be financially rewarded for killing a Jewish person, it wouldn't be long before all of the Jews would be hunted down and killed. Yet the whole time, nobody knew that the queen herself was a Jew, not even Haman, and the Jews themselves were kept in the dark. Then one Jew discovered the plot—and that person was none other than Mordecai, the one who had raised Esther, the queen, as a daughter.

A HEART OPEN TO CONCERN

So what happened next? The Bible gives a stirring account:

> When Mordecai learned of all that had been done, he tore his clothes, . . . and went out into the city, wailing loudly and bitterly. . . . When Esther's maids . . . came and told her about Mordecai, she was in great distress. . . . Esther summoned . . . one [who was] . . . assigned to attend her, and ordered him to find out what was troubling Mordecai and why. . . . Mordecai told him everything . . . including the exact amount of money Haman had promised to pay. . . . He also gave him a copy of the text of the edict . . . to show to Esther and explain it to her, and he told him to urge her to go into the king's presence to beg for mercy and plead with him for her people. (Esther 4:1, 4–5, 7–8)

Esther's first step on the path toward making history was opening her heart to concern. She made an effort to find out what was going on. She didn't turn away from what had been placed in front of her or pretend it wasn't there.

A thirty-year-old mother of six died in Miami, Florida on Wednesday, May 26, 1999. *But she didn't have to.* Stabbed and bleeding, she staggered from door to door, pleading for help, but nobody responded to her screams. She collapsed dead in a driveway. "You can only imagine the fear and anxiety she experienced, knowing that she was bleeding and dying and the frustration that she must have felt in trying to find someone to help her," noted police spokesman Lt. Bill Schwartz. Such incidents are not as infrequent as you might think. Thirty-eight people heard the screams of New York City resident Kitty Genovese and did nothing as she was stabbed to death.[1]

Such apathy does not mark great lives. A tourist followed Mother Teresa as she worked among the poor, unlovely, and destitute in the slums of Calcutta, India—easily one of the dankest cesspools in the world. They came upon an emaciated creature that used to be a man, hours from death, soiled, with running sores all over his body. As Mother Teresa bent down, picked the dying man up, cradled him in her arms, and lovingly, tenderly dressed a bloody, smelly, gaping hole where the leper's nose used to be, the tourist blurted out, "Mother Teresa, I wouldn't do what you're doing for ten million dollars."

"Neither would I," she answered, never taking her eyes off the man in her arms. "It's the love of Christ that moves me."[2]

You will never attempt great things for God or be used to accomplish great things for God unless you open your heart to concern—feeling what God feels, seeing what God sees, and caring about what God cares about.

COUNT THE COST OF INVOLVEMENT

After opening up her heart, Esther took the second step that anyone who makes history needs to take. She counted the cost of getting involved. "Then she instructed [her servant] to [return and] say to Mordecai, 'All the king's officials and the people of the royal provinces know that for any man or woman who approaches the king . . . without being summoned the king has but one law: that he be put to death'" (Esther 4:10–11).

It's not hard to relate to the young queen. "Okay, I see the problem, I see the need, but there is a pretty high cost for me if I get involved! I may lose my throne—I may even lose my life!" Everyone who has made the decision to surrender to God to be used to make a difference in the world could tell you of a moment when they came face to face with the *cost* involved. This is important, because unless you count the cost, you will never be committed.

Let's say you're offered a job, and you're led to believe that you'll have a corner office with a great view, a six-figure salary, and a company car. You take the job and then find out you're in a cubicle in the middle of the seventh floor. The salary is no different than your old job, and instead of a car, they give you a month's worth of bus tokens. You're out of there, right? But let's say you're approached by a startup company. They tell you that your office is going to be modest, they can only equal your present salary, and there aren't many perks. But you can get in on the ground floor of a promising business. You decide to take it. Then, when you get your modest office, base salary, and few if any perks, it's not that big of a deal. You *knew* it was going to be that way going *in*. When it happens, you don't bail. You stick with it. You've counted the cost, which means that you are much more able to be committed. That's why Jesus said that before anyone decides to come to Him as forgiver and leader, he or she should count the cost. He has no interest in limp-wristed, wimpy followers. He wants fully devoted, risk-taking kamikazes for the kingdom of God.

Yet sometimes counting the cost counts some people out. They see the price tag, the risk, and the inconvenience and say, "Sorry, God. I'm number one. I don't love or honor You enough to put You first. I'm not about to do anything that would affect the quality of my life. Take a risk? Sacrifice? Not in this life." Every time somebody counts the cost and comes out with that attitude, God has to look for another person to use. People who make a difference have not only counted the cost, they've *accepted* it. They're not afraid of the risk. They don't resent the sacrifice. They're not into living a *safe* life; they're into living a *significant* life.

Julia Roberts was catapulted into stardom through a series of early roles in movies such as *Mystic Pizza* and *Pretty Woman.* But it was another early film, *Steel Magnolias,* which explored the strength of a group of Southern women, that enabled her to give what was perhaps her most emotionally moving performance. In the film, Roberts plays a young girl by the name of Shelby, a newlywed who decides to get pregnant against the advice of her physician due to her diabetes. When Shelby tells her mother that she's pregnant, the moment of joy is marred by her mother's fury. She is livid that her daughter would risk her life in such a way, emotionally unwilling to trade the health of her child for the birth of a grandchild. Then Shelby responds. "Momma, don't you understand? I'd rather have thirty minutes of 'wonderful' than a lifetime of 'nothing special.'" A risk? Yes. But she knew it was the kind of risk that would make her life meaningful.

Far too many people are so busy trying to *protect* their lives that they never really *live* their lives. They stay in jobs that make them miserable, but they're afraid to take the risk of leaving. They don't draw close to people and reach out relationally, because they don't want to take the risk of getting hurt. They don't take on a new challenge or try something new, because they don't want to take the risk of failing. Result? A life of nothing special, when a life of *wonderful* was waiting to be experienced.

ALLOW YOURSELF TO BE CHALLENGED

There was a third step that Esther modeled, a step that is strategic. She allowed herself to be *challenged:*

> When Esther's words were reported to Mordecai, he sent back this answer: "Do not think that because you are in the king's house you alone of all the Jews will escape. For if you remain silent at this time, relief and deliverance for the Jews will arise from another place, but you and your father's family will perish. And who knows but that you have come to royal position for such a time as this?" (Esther 4:12–14)

Challenges surround us, but seldom do we allow them into our lives. If a church becomes too challenging, we drop out; if a mentor gets in our face, we no longer seek his counsel; if a position becomes too arduous, we simply resign and find a less strenuous role. Esther was the queen of Persia, with money, power, and fame. She didn't have to allow anyone to challenge her about anything in her life, not even the man who raised her. *But she did.* People who allow themselves to be challenged, like Esther, are the ones who make a difference with their lives. Why? *We all tend to rise to the degree that we are challenged.*

I once heard of a man who climbed to the top of his field and was relatively well known in his community and state. One day he was asked the secret of his success. He said that as a child, he was swimming in a lake one afternoon, all alone. Suddenly, he suffered severe cramps and couldn't swim or even stay afloat. Just as he was about to drown, he felt a man's strong arm lifting him up out of the water.

Once on shore, all he could think to say was, "Thank you, sir, for saving my life."

"You're welcome, son," the man replied. "See to it that you were worth saving."[3]

If you are a Christian, you have been saved—now shouldn't you see to it that you were worth saving? I don't mean in terms of earning your salvation or walking away from the idea of grace. None of us were worth saving, and we can do nothing to earn it. But as Dietrich Bonhoeffer wrote in his classic book *The Cost of Discipleship,* grace should never be cheap. It came at too high a price to the One Who purchased it.

I was deeply impacted by the Academy Award-winning movie *Saving Private Ryan*. The story centers around a man, Private Ryan, who lost three brothers. The army considered that such a loss to a single family that a group of soldiers, led by a captain played by Tom Hanks, was sent in to find Private Ryan and bring him home. In the end, Ryan was found and rescued, but not before the captain himself—along with many others—had been killed. His dying words to the young private, reflecting on all that had been done to save him and get him home, were simply, "Earn it."

The film then flashes forward to the present day. Private Ryan, near the end of his life, looks at the grave of that captain and becomes overwhelmed with emotion at the thought of the sacrifice that went into saving him. He turns to his wife and says, "Tell me I'm a good man. That I've lived a good life." *Tell me that I really did earn it.* At the end of his life, that's what mattered most. It's what will matter the most to all of us.

MAKE HISTORY

This leads to the fourth step that Esther took, a step that made all of the difference in the world. She had opened her heart to concern, she had counted the cost, and she had allowed her life to be challenged. Mordecai had told her that this was her moment! He had challenged her to do something significant with her life. God's purposes would prevail, and if she didn't come through, God would search the land and find someone who would, but right now that person could be her! Esther's response? "I will go to the

king, even though it is against the law. And if I perish, I perish"
(Esther 4:16). That is the fourth and final step: You do what God
wants you to do. You do what would honor Him. You say yes,
regardless of the cost.

This is a rare and remarkable spirit. I'll never forget coming
across a photo that was taken in 1978 when President Carter
attempted to reinstate draft registration. What stuck with me had
nothing to do with the draft. The photo was of a young Princeton
student who carried a poster that said, "Nothing is worth dying
for." So many in our world are represented by that sentiment, that
nothing is worth dying for. They lead lives devoid of passion,
empty of conviction. But until you have something that you
would die for, you don't have anything to live for. As one of this
country's greatest leaders, President Theodore Roosevelt, said:

> It is not the critic who counts, not the man who points out
> how the strong man stumbled, or where the doer of deeds
> could have done them better. The credit belongs to the man
> who is actually in the arena; whose face is marred by dust and
> sweat and blood; who strives valiantly; who errs and comes
> short again and again; who knows the great enthusiasms, the
> great devotions, and spends himself in a worthy cause; who,
> at best, knows in the end the triumph of high achievement;
> and who, at the worst, if he fails, at least fails while daring
> greatly, so that his place shall never be with those cold and
> timid souls who know neither victory nor defeat.[4]

The entire course of your life will be determined by whether you will do what God wants you to do. You have been given a purpose. Now fulfill it! Serve where He wants you to serve; give what He wants you to give. God's grand purposes in this world will prevail—with or without you—but this could be your moment! You could be the one He uses!

No one really knows for sure, of course, but here's a little theory I have. There was going to be an evangelical movement that would result in crusades and colleges, publications and ministries, but it didn't have to involve a young North Carolina farm boy by the name of Billy Graham. There was going to be a ministry to families that would turn countless hearts toward the home, but it didn't have to be championed by a California psychologist named James Dobson. There was going to be a number of widely influential new churches started to spark a movement toward the vision of the New Testament church, but it didn't have to involve Bill Hybels. Yet each of these people has made history, because each said yes to God. As Os Guinness once observed, "Too often Christianity has not been tried and found wanting; it has been found demanding and not tried."[5]

Esther faced the demands and gave it her life. Want to know how her story turned out? When she went to the king, he didn't kill her. When he found out what was going on, he killed Haman! Then he took Mordecai and elevated him to a place of honor. As a result, the Jewish people were saved—the people who one day would produce a man named Jesus, the very Savior of the world.

IN THE NAME OF CHRIST

I've got a feeling that most of us would like to be makers of history. We want our lives to add up to something significant, to be part of something that will live on long after we are gone. The good news is that it isn't just important people in decisive situations who are able to be used by God to make a difference with their lives. The record reveals that the vast majority of God's most instrumental activity has been through ordinary people being faithful in everyday situations. People like you and me. Our lives, lived on purpose, can cause ripples that will never cease.[6]

In the fourth century, an Asiatic monk named Telemachus spent most of his life in a remote community of prayer, raising vegetables for the cloister kitchen. Then one day this little monk felt that God wanted him to go to Rome, the capital of the world, the busiest, wealthiest, biggest city on earth. Telemachus had no idea why God wanted him to go there, and he was absolutely terrified at the thought. But as he prayed, he knew that he was supposed to go. So he went.

When he arrived at the city with a little sack on his back holding everything he owned, Telemachus encountered a huge throng of people moving toward the largest building he had ever seen: a coliseum. What he didn't know was that the crowd was going to see the gladiator contests. Telemachus joined them, not knowing what was in store and still searching for the purposes of God.

As he took his seat, Telemachus saw the great warriors march into the arena, salute the emperor, and shout, "We who are about to die, salute you!" He soon realized that this huge crowd of people had come to cheer men on to murder one another—human lives for entertainment. As the horror of the moment enveloped him, the little monk jumped up in his seat and shouted, "In the name of Christ, *stop!*"

The fighting began, of course. No one could hear the voice of the little monk. Telemachus was undaunted. He ran down the stone steps and bounded onto the sandy floor of the arena. The crowd shouted and cheered as the little man in a monk's robe ran back and forth between the fighters. They assumed he was a part of the entertainment. Almost playfully, a gladiator took his shield and batted little Telemachus away from his legs. The crowd laughed.

But Telemachus got up and ran back between the fighters, shouting, "In the name of Christ, *stop!*" No longer was this seen as amusing. Telemachus was obstructing the games and interfering with the contests. The crowd began to yell, "Run him through! Run him through!" Dutifully, a gladiator took his sword and slashed into the stomach of the little monk.

The crowd grew strangely quiet. As he died, lying in his own blood, Telemachus said once more, "In the name of Christ, *stop.*" This time, everyone heard his words. Then a strange thing occurred. Whether it was the utter shock of his own actions or the conviction of the dead monk's words, as the two gladiators and the crowd focused on the still form on the sandy floor, someone in the top tier of the arena got up and walked out. Another followed. Then another. Soon, all over the arena, people began to leave, until the huge stadium was empty. That was the last gladiatorial contest in the Roman coliseum. Never again did men kill each other for the crowd's entertainment on those grounds.[7]

Telemachus was used by God to become a maker of history.

You can be the agent and instrument of God's great plan. God doesn't care if you are educated or illiterate, black or white, rich or poor, male or female, young or old. All He wants to know is if you are going to open your heart to concern, if you will count the cost in order to be committed, if you will allow yourself to be challenged, and if you will then do what He wants you to do selflessly and sacrificially. If so, then God will take you in His mighty right hand and use you to change the world.

But if not—if you're hardening your heart, walking away from commitment, refusing to be challenged, and ignoring what God would have you to do—then I beg you, in the name of Christ, *stop*. Life is too short, God's mission is too important, and what you can give is too significant. Most people go to their graves with their music still inside them.[8] Don't let that be your story. Instead, make the effort to live the life God intended for you—*a purposeful life*.

About the Author

James Emery White is the founding and senior pastor of Mecklenburg Community Church in Charlotte, North Carolina. His previous books include *Rethinking the Church, A Search for the Spiritual,* and *You Can Experience . . . A Spiritual Life.* Jim and his wife, Susan, live in Charlotte with their four children: Rebecca, Rachel, Jonathan, and Zachary.

Endnotes

Chapter One: The Life You Long For

1. Adapted from John Sculley, *Odyssey* (New York: Harper & Row, 1987), 56-91.

2. As cited by Tony Campolo, *Who Switched the Price Tags?* (Waco: Word, 1986), 28-29.

3. The most famous hierarchy of human drives was put forward by Abraham Maslow, working from the base of physiological needs, all the way up to what he termed "self-actualization." The more popularly stated form I have used is far from original with me, but I am unsure of its original source. It was first suggested to my thinking by Rick Warren's use of it in "The Purpose Driven Life, Part 1," delivered at Saddleback Valley Community Church, Lake Forest, California, April 17-18, 1993.

4. John Naisbitt, *Megatrends* (New York: Warner, 1982), 231-47.

5. Lewis Carroll, *Alice's Adventures in Wonderland* (New York: Alfred A. Knopf, 1984), 89.

6. Harold Begbie, *The Life of General Wm Booth* (New York: Macmillan, 1920), 422.

7. Adapted from Chuck Colson and Jack Eckerd, *Why America Doesn't Work* (Dallas: Word, 1991), xii.

8. As cited by Norman Rose in *Churchill: The Unruly Giant* (New York: The Free Press, 1994), 329.

9. This story is told by Mike Vance, the original dean of Disney University, and has been adapted from his retelling by Tom Paterson in *Living the Life You Were Meant to Live* (Nashville: Thomas Nelson, 1998), 254-55.

Chapter Two: What It Means to Be Human

1. Robert Wells, *Is a Blue Whale the Biggest Thing There Is?* (Morton Grove, Ill.: Albert Whitman & Co., 1993).

2. This opening material has been adapted from Robert Jastrow, *God and the Astronomers,* 2nd ed. (New York: W. W. Norton, 1992), 10-11.

3. Tony Campolo, *Everything You've Ever Heard Is Wrong* (Dallas: Word, 1992), 31-32.

4. Sir Fred Hoyle, *The Intelligent Universe* (London: Michael Joseph, 1983), 11-12, 19, 251. For a recent presentation of the inescapability of some form of intelligent design, see Michael J. Behe, *Darwin's Black Box: The Biochemical Challenge to Evolution* (New York: The Free Press, 1996).

5. Stephen Hawking, quoted by John Boslough, *Masters of Time: Cosmology at the End of Innocence* (New York: Addison-Wesley Publishing Company, 1992), 55.

6. Stephen Hawking, *A Brief History of Time* (New York: Bantam, 1988), 127.

7. As quoted by Luis Palau, *God Is Relevant* (New York: Doubleday, 1997), 32.

8. Paul Davies, *The Mind of God* (New York: Simon and Schuster, 1992), 232. For more on the various scientific supports for the creation and design of human life, see the author's *A Search for the Spiritual* (Grand Rapids: Baker, 1998).

9. This analogy was brought to my attention in Tony Campolo's *Carpe Diem* (Dallas: Word, 1995), 130. For more on Kierkegaard's thought, see *Fear and Trembling* (New York: Penguin, 1985) and *The Sickness Unto Death* (New York: Penguin, 1989).

10. Adapted from Heather Whitestone, "Listening with My Heart," *Crossings Corner,* September 1997, 2; and Rebecca Price Janney, *Great Stories in American History* (Camp Hill: Horizon, 1998), 177-78.

11. Os Guinness, *The Call* (Nashville: Word, 1998), 31.

12. C. S. Lewis, *Mere Christianity* (New York: Macmillan, 1952), 140.

13. From Os Guinness, *The Dust of Death* (Downers Grove: InterVarsity, 1973), 148.

14. Adapted from Mary Ann Bird, *The Whisper Test,* as cited by Les Parrott in *High-Maintenance Relationships* (Wheaton: Tyndale, 1996), 206.

15. John Gray, *Men Are from Mars, Women Are from Venus* (New York: HarperCollins, 1992).

16. Tom Paterson, *Living the Life You Were Meant to Live* (Nashville: Thomas Nelson, 1998), 5.

17. As quoted in Michael Scammell, *Solzhenitsyn: A Biography* (New York: W. W. Norton, 1984), 340.

18. Gordon MacDonald, *The Effective Father* (Wheaton: Tyndale, 1977), 183-184.

19. This story has been told by Craddock himself, but it has also been retold by Tony Campolo in an address I heard him deliver to Southern Seminary in Louisville, Kentucky. I've borrowed richly from both in my own presentation, using Craddock's content and some of Campolo's style and injected humor.

Chapter Three: Examining the Call of God

1. Adapted from Tim Stafford, *That's Not What I Meant* (Grand Rapids: Zondervan, 1995), 7-9.

2. Our new identities in Christ, and the purposes they entail, are found throughout the New Testament and have been the basis for many talks, books, and study guides. This chapter was particularly served by a sermon series taught by Bill Hybels at Willow Creek Community Church in South Barrington, Illinois, as well as a subsequent study guide: *The Real You: Discovering Your Identity in Christ/Interactions Small Group Series* (Grand Rapids: Zondervan/Willow Creek Resources, 1996).

3. Adapted from Campolo, *Who Switched the Price Tags?*, 195-96.

4. Lewis, *Mere Christianity,* 174.

5. For help on this, see the author's *You Can Experience a Spiritual Life.*

6. Adapted from Gordon MacDonald, *Rebuilding Your Broken World* (Nashville: Thomas Nelson, 1988), 92.

7. On the life of Franks, see Tom Clancy, *Into the Storm: A Study in Military Command* (New York: G. P. Putnam's Sons, 1997).

8. Adapted from Charles Swindoll, *Improving Your Serve* (Waco: Word, 1981), 46-47.

9. Michael Green, *Evangelism in the Early Church* (Grand Rapids: Eerdmans, 1970), 173.

10. Adapted from "On Courage" in *Chicken Soup for the Soul,* written and compiled by Jack Canfield and Mark Victor Hansen (Deerfield Beach, FL: Health Communications, Inc., 1993), 27-28.

11. Adapted from Campolo, *Who Switched the Price Tags?,* 33-34.

Chapter Four: Determining Your Values

1. Adapted from Bill and Kathy Peel, *Discover Your Destiny* (Colorado Springs: NavPress, 1996), 162.

2. Adapted from Campolo, *Carpe Diem,* 178-79.

3. Statistics presented by *The New York Times,* August 24, 1997, as cited by *The Pastor's Weekly Briefing,* August 29, 1997 (Vol. 5, No. 35), 2.

4. These figures have most certainly grown since they were first reported by George Barna in *The Frog in the Kettle: What Christians Need to Know About Life in the Year 2000* (Ventura: Regal, 1990), 53.

5. As quoted by Fred Fedler, *An Introduction to the Mass Media* (New York: Harcourt Brace Jovanovich, Inc., 1978), 8.

6. On this, see James Fallows, *Breaking the News: How the Media Undermine American Democracy* (New York: Pantheon Books, 1996).

7. "Some perspective, please," *WORLD*, September 20, 1997 (Vol. 12, No. 18), 9.

8. Ibid.

9. For an intriguing overview of how people and events can be placed into a certain perspective, regardless of fact, see the work edited by Mark C. Carnes, *Past Imperfect: History According to the Movies* (New York: Henry Hold and Company, 1995).

10. Jim Impoco, "TV's Frisky Family Values," *U.S. News & World Report*, April 15, 1996 (Vol. 120, No. 15), 58-62.

11. Ibid.

12. As cited by Michael Medved, *Hollywood vs. America* (New York: HarperCollins, 1992), 271.

13. For the insights of Schaeffer, see *The Complete Works of Francis A. Schaeffer*, Volumes 1-5 (Westchester: Crossway, 1982).

14. As cited by Robert H. Frank, Luxury Fever: *Why Money Fails to Satisfy in an Era of Excess* (New York: Free Press, 1999), 4.

15. Taken from William Martin, *A Prophet with Honor: The Billy Graham Story* (New York: William Morrow, 1991), 112.

16. Adapted from Maxwell, *Developing the Leader within You,* 37.

Chapter Five: Discovering Your Strengths

1. The idea of gifts being part of your spiritual "DNA" is far from original with me and can be found in many writings on the subject. Using the letters as an acrostic in the manner I have designed is, however, my own application.

2. For more on this, see Arthur F. Miller, Jr., *Why You Can't Be Anything You Want to Be* (Grand Rapids: Zondervan, 1999).

3. Adapted from Virginia Cowles, *Winston Churchill: The Era and the Man* (New York: Grossett and Dunlap, 1953), 32. The story is built on the recollections of Churchill's cousin.

4. There are a number of good resources available on the subject of spiritual gifts, such as Bruce Bugbee's *What You Do Best in the Body of Christ* (Grand Rapids: Zondervan, 1995).

5. My personal favorite is *Networking* (Zondervan/Willow Creek Resources), because it not only helps you investigate your spiritual gifts, but incorporates passions and personality type as well.

6. Adapted from Luciano Pavarotti, *Pavarotti: My Own Story* (Garden City: Doubleday, 1981).

7. These four personality category divergences have been adapted from several sources, including *Please Understand Me: Character and Temperament Types* by David Kiersey and

Marilyn Bates (Del Mar, CA: Prometheus Nemesis Book Company, 1978/1984), and Bill Hybels adaptation of the Kiersey-Bates categories in *Honest to God* (Grand Rapids: Zondervan, 1990), 70-73. Both pull from the famous Myers-Brigg categories. I have leaned most heavily on Bill's popularization of the Kiersey-Bates material.

8. On this, see Tom Paterson, *Living the Life You Were Meant to Live* (Nashville: Thomas Nelson, 1998), and Os Guinness, *The Call* (Nashville: Word, 1998).

9. Adapted from "A Change in Jobs, Thought," by Pauline Jelinek, Associated Press, as printed in *The Charlotte Observer,* Thursday, April 1, 1999, 2A.

10. Paterson, *Living the Life You Were Meant to Live,* 21.

11. Dorothy Sayers, *Creed or Chaos* (New York: Harcourt, Brace, 1949), 53.

12. Adapted from Campolo, *Who Switched the Price Tags?,* 158-60.

Chapter Six: Defining Your Mission

1. David Perlmutt, "Inspired by Games," *The Charlotte Observer* (Wednesday, July 31, 1996), 1C, 5C.

2. Adapted from Campolo, *Carpe Diem,* 40.

3. James C. Collins in a talk given in Chicago at The Leadership Summit, August 1997.

4. I cannot locate the source from which I first adapted the retelling of this event, but the dialogue and events are as reported.

5. Adapted from Campolo, *Everything You've Ever Heard Is Wrong,* 17.

6. See A. L. Williams, *All You Can Do Is All You Can Do* (Nashville: Thomas Nelson, 1988), 74-76.

7. Adapted from Campolo, *Who Switched the Price Tags?,* 69-72.

8. This was adapted from an address given by Billy Graham at InterVarsity Christian Fellowship's 1981 Urbana Convention.

9. Theodore Roszak, *The Making of a Counter Culture* (New York: Anchor Books, 1969), 43-44.

10. Adapted from personal accounts of the story from Bill himself, as well as the recording of the event in Bill and Lynne Hybels's book, *Rediscovering Church* (Grand Rapids: Zondervan, 1995), 166-67.

11. Adapted from Swindoll, *Improving Your Serve,* 127-28.

Chapter Seven: Ordering Your World

1. As chronicled by Daniel J. Boorstin, *The Americans: The Democratic Experience* (New York: Vintage Books, 1974), 596.

2. This famous sentence was transmitted to earth as "one small step for man" instead of "a man" due to transmission difficulties. Armstrong's actual words were "a man," though the "a" was never heard.

3. On this, see James C. Collins and Jerry I. Porras, *Built to Last: Successful Habits of Visionary Companies* (New York: HarperCollins, 1994).

4. Gordon MacDonald, *Ordering Your Private World* (Chicago: Moody, 1984), 81-86.

5. Ibid., 84-85.

6. Adapted from Tim Hansel's *When I Relax I Feel Guilty* (Elgin: David C. Cook, 1979), 67.

7. Adapted from Charles Swindoll, *Strengthening Your Grip* (Waco: Word, 1982), 99-100.

8. Adapted from Maxwell, *Developing the Leader within You,* 25-26.

9. Of course, there are some exceptions. Neither your DNA nor your sense of mission should prevent the call to servanthood when needs of a general nature present themselves before you. My life-mission is not directed toward mopping floors, but it is a task I currently perform with my family as part of a serving team at my church. Boundaries should never be used as an excuse not to serve in a general, "community" sense.

10. As recorded by William J. Bennett, *The Book of Virtues* (New York: Simon and Schuster, 1993), 198-200.

Chapter Eight: Maximizing Your Impact

1. For more on how to maintain a vital union with Christ, see the author's *You Can Experience a Spiritual Life.*

2. James Emery White, *Rethinking the Church* (Grand Rapids: Baker, 1997), 33.

3. Adapted from Swindoll, *Strengthening Your Grip,* 205-206.

4. The following section has been developed from the author's

You Can Experience a Spiritual Life, 112-13, though in a very abridged form. For a fuller treatment of how relationships can impact a spiritual life, the entire section should be consulted.

5. Adapted from Max Lucado, *He Still Moves Stones* (Dallas: Word, 1993), 101-102.

6. As quoted by Maxwell, *Developing the Leader within You,* 145.

7. Michael Jordan, *I Can't Accept Not Trying* (New York: HarperCollins, 1994), 14-15.

8. Doug Sherman and William Hendricks, *How to Balance Competing Time Demands* (Colorado Springs: NavPress, 1989), 39.

9. As cited by Denis Waitley, *Being the Best* (Nashville: Thomas Nelson, 1987), 163.

10. Adapted from the national airing by NBC-TV of the 1998 Hawaiian Open Ironman Triathlon, rebroadcast on Sunday, July 25, 1999.

11. Adapted from Tim Hansel, *Holy Sweat* (Waco: Word, 1987), 131.

12. Adapted from Lawson, *Men Who Win,* 96-97.

Chapter Nine: Following God's Lead

1. C. S. Lewis, *God in the Dock* (Grand Rapids: Eerdmans, 1970), 105.

2. Adapted from Garry Friesen and J. Robin Maxson, *Principles for Decision Making* (Portland: Multnomah Press, 1984), 11-13. See also their longer treatment of the subject

in *Decision Making and the Will of God* (Portland: Multnomah, 1980).

3. Adapted from M. Blaine Smith, *Knowing God's Will* (Downers Grove: InterVarsity Press, 1991), 59-60.

4. Adapted from Paul Little, *Affirming the Will of God* (Downers Grove: InterVarsity Press, 1971), 28-29.

5. As cited by Smith, *Knowing God's Will,* 91.

6. Adapted from Charles Swindoll, *The Tale of the Tardy Oxcart* (Nashville: Word, 1998), 246.

7. Paul Johnson, *Intellectuals* (New York: Harper and Row, 1988).

8. Adapted from Craig Brian Larson, editor, *Illustrations for Preaching and Teaching* (Grand Rapids: Baker, 1993), 148.

Chapter Ten: Becoming a Maker of History

1. Adapted from an Associated Press article (no author cited), "Woman Dies After Cries for Help Ignored," *The Charlotte Observer,* May 27, 1999, section 6A.

2. Adapted from Nancy L. Darner, *God's Vitamin "C" for the Spirit,* compiled by Kathy Collard Miller and D. Larry Miller (Lancaster, Penn.: Starburst, 1996), 20.

3. Source unknown.

4. As quoted by John Maxwell, *The 21 Irrefutable Laws of Leadership* (Nashville: Thomas Nelson, 1998), 28-29.

5. Guinness, *The Dust of Death,* 359.

6. Ibid., 390.

7. Adapted from Charles Colson, *Loving God* (Grand Rapids: Zondervan, 1983), 241-43.

8. Oliver Wendell Holmes, as quoted by Peel, *Discover Your Destiny*, 9.

I want to experience a spiritual life...
but where do I start?

Experience the spiritual life you've longed for

The first book in a series that addresses your spiritual concerns, *You Can Experience...A Spiritual Life* shows you how to meet the needs of your questioning heart. With a fresh, straightforward style, author and pastor James Emery White gives real life examples to inspire and encourage you to know more about how to live as a Christian.